IT'S ABOUT YOUR CAREER

Skills For a Lifetime of Loving Your Work!

by Ryland Leyton

It's About Your Career

Skills For a Lifetime of Loving Your Work!

By Ryland Leyton

ISBN: 978-0-578-60404-6

Dedication

This book is dedicated to

- The managers who put up with me having to learn so much from direct experience;

- The family, friends, and colleagues who helped me over the rough patches; and

- The people who gave me opportunities and encouragement.

I hope this book both honors and "pays forward" your investment in me.

Table of Contents

Preface

Why I Wrote This Book

At the time I'm writing this, I have been in the working world for about 25 years. I've changed careers a few times. I have gone from being horribly naive and unsophisticated about how to get a job and what to expect from an employer to believing I may be a successfully functioning adult. (Although opinions may vary about that. Just ask a few of my supervisors.)

I have learned some lessons along the way. Some were easy, some hard. Some were *very* hard.

That last group cost me a lot—in money, in reputation, in time spent backtracking along a wrong path I'd taken or, a few times, rebuilding an opportunity that I'd lost. Once or twice, this time was measured in years.

I would like to spare you these costs if I can.

I would like to offer you the opportunity to learn from my experiences, if they are helpful to you.

I would like to honor and appreciate the excellent teachers and mentors that I have been fortunate to know—both personal and professional—by attempting to pass on the wisdom, caring, and support they gave me.

My wish and hope for you

Follow your passion, take pride in your work, deliver great value, and always do the right thing. Be happy, satisfied, and proud of your career as a whole.

Care for and respect your workplace, your coworkers, your supervisor, and especially anyone for whom you have responsibility. Treat your customers well.

Do powerful and wonderful things at work, contribute to the company, and grow your skills, your abilities, and yourself as a person.

Enable and support other people along their journey to accomplish these same things.

Introduction

Who Should Read This Book?

This book is for you if any of the following statements describe you:

- You are actively interested in nurturing your career.

- You want to be happy with your career choices.

- You are seeking a framework that will help you get from *here* to *there.*

- You want to explore the options in your professional future.

- You are trying to provide some homemade structure to your career.

- You want to look back in 10 years and say, "I made some good choices."

- You want to find the career of your dreams and love your work!

In short, if you are seeking a happy, rewarding, and fulfilling career, this book is for you.

Today's workplace lacks career guidance

There's a lot of conversation in professional circles about different generations working together; we have baby boomers, Generation Xers, Millennials, and most recently, Generation Zers. There are interesting resources online about the generational differences in focus, communication styles, and inherent skills, and how each of these groups can manage (or be managed by) the others.

What is missing from the conversation is the aspect of growing and developing talent within the workforce and across generations. This should happen at the one-to-one level of the supervisor and supervisee, and I find that is largely missing in the workplace today.

These skills are seldom inborn in managers of any stripe, and they cannot pass on what they do not know. This complicates an already difficult problem: how do you manage your own career—a responsibility no one can abdicate—when even your manager can't guide and advise you? I've had conversations with people in their 20s to 50s, and even some considering continuing their career into retirement, in which one or more of these themes consistently crop up:

- My manager isn't helping my career.

- My company doesn't seem to care if I develop or not.

- I'm not sure what to do to get promoted.

- I'm not sure if this company is a long- or short-term thing for me.

- I feel like I don't have the training or guidance to be successful in my career.

- I don't know what career paths exist or how to create one for myself.

This tells me that people often get lost when navigating their careers around the various obstacles and rapids on the river of life, deciding what shore to stop on and when to pick up and go again. Frequently the people above them lack the skill to help, or cannot communicate the help in a way the individual can receive. Sometimes that help is just not relevant because the pace of change has increased so rapidly. Even Millennials and Generation Z will someday be in the position of confusion and change-resistance they now scorn in those older than themselves.

Everyone faces these issues.

This book can help

I have tried to write this book from a place that is neutral with respect to technology, generation, or specific parenting and work environments.

That's why this approach works across generations: it omits irrelevant externalities and homes in on your *values*. Knowing what is important to you—understanding what priority work has in your own life and the value of your career *for yourself*—is a foundation from which anyone can start.

Life, work, and everything

Work is a great thing, but it is often only *one* thing in your life.

In this book, I'm going to be talking mostly about work and career. Please understand that I know this is *not* the only thing in life.

One slightly tongue-in-cheek way of saying this is that your whole life might be made up of differing proportions of:

- Family

- Faith

- Fitness

- Friends

- Fun

- Finance

We all have only so much energy. No matter how much energy you have, you have the same 24 hours in a day that everyone else gets.

Figure 1: Work in the context of life

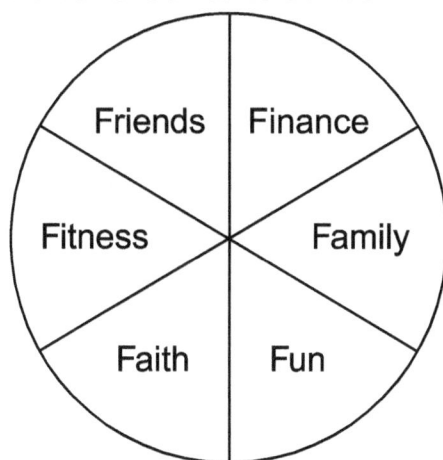

Work is an important part of life, but not the only important part!

Your career ("finance") may get more or less of your attention and energy at different times in your life. The same could be said of the rest of these areas. Sometimes an area will pop up unexpectedly—as frequently happens with family, friends, or fitness (health). These things take what they take, when they take it. Sometimes we have to choose between them.

As an easy example, I know someone who had the opportunity to make a significant career advancement, if they were willing to make the investment of time and attention. At the same time, they had recently divorced and had retained custody of their high-school-aged children, who would both be going off to college over the next three years.

This person made a conscious and intentional choice: they would pass up the career opportunity and actively spend time with the kids and their family-centric sports hobbies until they went to college, knowing that this time would not come again.

Similarly, I know people who take jobs that involve extensive travel and extra hours early in their careers, to have these experiences before it is important to them to settle down. The lack of attachments lets them spend the extra time with their careers in ways that don't require compromise or consent from other people. Most of these people eventually get tired of this and want to shift in the other direction, and of course that's fine, too.

Remember, your workplace will not meet all your needs. If you have a great profession that enables great things in your life, and your passion is somewhere else—with your family, your house, or your artwork—that is just fine.

This book is primarily about the workplace and the activities of managing your career, but there is much more to life than work.

If you can work in the Zone of Awesome, why wouldn't you?

What would it take for your work to be awesome?

This is one of my favorite pictures when talking about work.

Let's spend a few minutes with this.

The four main circles are, clockwise from the top:

- That which you love

- That which the world needs

- That which you can be paid for

- That which you are good at

I think these are self-explanatory.

The important thing is to try to live at the middle of this diagram when you can, in what I've labeled the "Zone of Awesome."

In my humble opinion, especially when talking about the world of work and careers, if you can exist at the middle point of all the circles—doing something you love that benefits the world, which you are paid for and you are good at—why would you ever *not* do this?

Let's shoot for that spot!

It can take time to find, or build, your own "awesome"

It is rare we land in the "Zone of Awesome" early or immediately in our career. This is simply never an overnight or sudden thing. It takes time to build. There is a lot of learning involved.

Can you imagine that all of these are true immediately in life?

- You know what you love doing and what drives you.

- It is something that permits you to make the living you want.

- You have strong skills in this area.

- This thing you love produces a societal benefit.

Even if those things are true, it is almost impossible that you have a lot of *experience* at it as well.

You must expect time, learning, and experiences to influence you. This isn't sudden.

In writing this book I've tried to help you develop a road map—that you can update!—to get you to your own unique Zone of Awesome!

If you can't work in the Zone of Awesome—or at least you can't right away, but you're building to it for later in your career—let's talk about what the other locations need.

Mission is that which you love *and* which the world needs. You're not necessarily good at it, nor is anyone (currently) paying you for it. These are activities that you spend time doing because they feel good to you, and other people receive value when you do them. These are typically charitable, artistic, spiritual, or service activities, which benefit another person or people in some way.

Vocation is that which the world needs *and* which you can be paid for. Regardless of whether you love it, hopefully you can be good at it—hey, you are getting paid, here!—but that is not required. Many people do jobs that someone else needs done . . . but perhaps they are simply adequate (not excellent) at the job.

Profession is that which you can be paid for *and* which you are good at. This is the thing you're doing, you're good at doing, and hopefully you're making a decent living doing. Note that "you love it" is still not part of the equation. We all know people like this: the superb doctor who really wants to be an artist; the CEO who would rather be a pastor.

Passion is that which you are good at doing *and* which you love. No one is paying you for it, and the world may be indifferent to it. As with a mission, a passion may be artistic, spiritual, or service oriented—the difference is that you are good at your passion and you invest personally in developing your skills.

Note that there are small, unlabeled spaces where three of our circles overlap. In each of these, our adjustment is simple: just add one of the missing things. It never makes the situation worse!

Do you have a job, or a career?

The workplace is not just a job: don't think of it that way. Do not deny yourself the canvas and potential experience that the workplace gives you.

Compare these two different approaches to a job at a hypothetical company:

> *Job thinking*—I'm going to work at Widget Company. I have a job as a salesperson in the Widget Company Showroom. I talk to customers who are interested in buying the widgets we sell. I get paid every other week, and my pay includes a bonus for sales I've been part of every three months.

> *Career thinking*—I'm going to work at Widget Company. Widget company makes widgets. My position is to sell widgets at the Town Center Widget Showroom. Widget Company has been in business for about 15 years. Building and outfitting the Widget Showroom in the shopping center I work in cost the company $5 million. The building and staff here represent an investment of $1 million per month. There are entire organizations in Widget Company whose roles are to supply the store where I work with widgets, to hire me and the people to manage me, to make sure we get paid, to make sure our phones work, and to maintain the store. There are people who develop the new widget for the next year, and who train me on how to sell it. A lot of money and effort have gone into creating this place in which I'll work.

Two very different perspectives, right? But the difference between them is even bigger than it may seem.

Let's go back and add the following statement to the end of each of the preceding "thinking" paragraphs:

> At this place, I'll do my job and live my values. Along the way, I'll make contributions, learn from other people, and make the difference that I can make.

To me, this makes the difference much more striking. These are two *totally* different canvases and ways of thinking about your work.

I like to say we all contribute to making a great place to work. You may think it's only up to management; *it is not*. You can contribute to your workplace just by clipping an inoffensive, funny newspaper cartoon and posting it in the breakroom for people to see unexpectedly. It may surprise someone, make them laugh, and you'll have contributed to other people having a good day.

You've probably heard of Maslow's hierarchy of needs (figure 3)

Figure 3: Maslow's hierarchy of needs

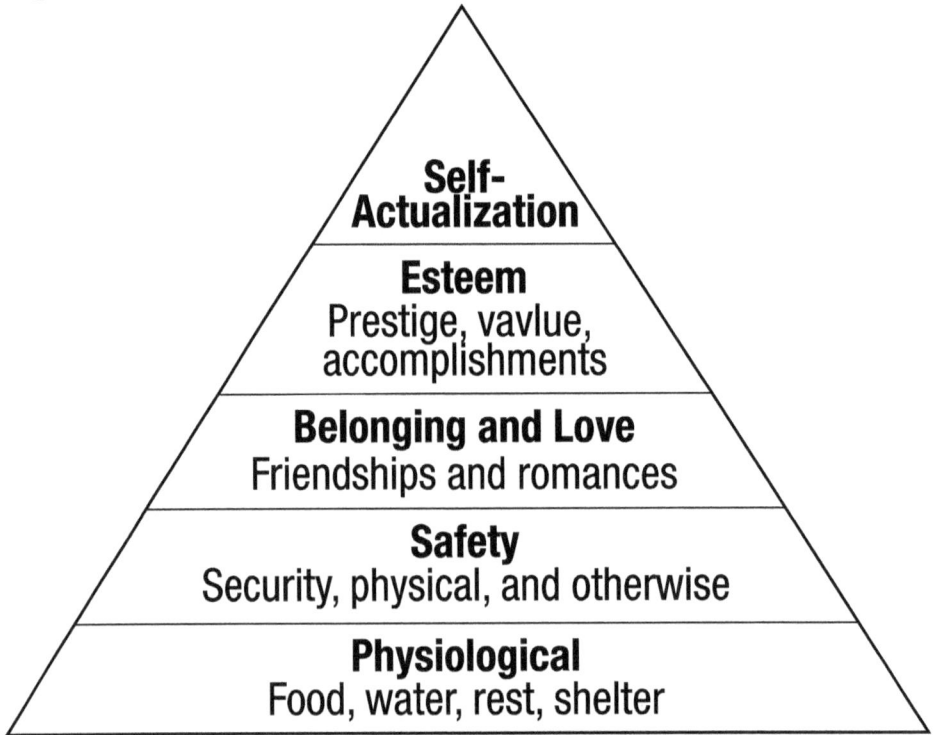

Your workplace can play a big part in all of your basic needs.

Let's pretend that your food, shelter, and other physical and safety needs are met. Work is probably contributing to both of these levels through funding for your home and other parts of the physicality of living.

But what about the levels above? We tend to think of those as having more to do with the realms of home, family, close friends, and inner self, but the workplace contributes to these levels as well.

Belonging and love needs: Work friendships and colleagues are important—certainly they count as relationships, or we wouldn't invest so much in them!

Esteem needs: Typically, work occupies tons of our time, and our esteem, prestige, and accomplishment derive at least somewhat from our workplace. We certainly want to be seen as competent at our job!

Self-actualization: Achieving our full potential, being creative, being generative—all of these are relevant at work as well.

Remember, life is bigger than work! At the same time, look at the canvas that work offers you to do things that are truly important to you: build relationships, create accomplishments, and achieve your potential.

I'm not saying you should overinvest at work; I *am* saying that you shouldn't look at most work as just a J-O-B—instead, realize what potential it has and decide whether what you're doing now is the right fit for you. Let's ensure you find the right fit for your values and interests, and see if your work can be in the Zone of Awesome!

How to use this book

This book has three parts:

Vision—Exploring your values, making goals, identifying gaps, making an action plan

Job hunting skills—Concrete and practical things to do for your resume and during interviews

Advice from the ages—Career advice I've been fortunate to receive from mentors and learn from experience

Part 1: Vision, goals, and plans

Part 1 will guide you through an exercise to surface your values regarding the workplace and identify goals that align with those values. We will position work in the context of your whole life and identify goals, as well as actions to help you achieve those goals. This section is heavily introspective, and you may revisit it several times for various personal reasons as your perspective changes over time.

Part 2: Job hunting skills

In Part 2 we go into detail about the interview process. We discuss resumes, interview types and skills, and all the preparation that goes into getting ready to talk with someone about the position. This includes your career story—a way of helping you connect with your interviewer—and the STAR answer format—a great way to respond to interview questions. I also discuss ways of considering the options that are presented to you as you go through the offer-and-acceptance process.

Part 3: Lessons and gifts

Part 3 is composed of short essays in which I pass along lessons I have learned. Some of these lessons come directly from my experience, some I've been lucky to have learned from others. Hopefully a few of these will be useful, or at least interesting. At the very least they will provide an opportunity to have a good-natured laugh with my younger self.

Worksheets

I have included worksheets, with some examples, at the end of the book. I encourage you to register at RylandLeyton.com for access to updates as I make them.

Sequence and flow of your reading

I recommend that you read these chapters in order the first time. This book isn't very long, and I think reading straight through will help you organize your thinking.

Later, you may revisit your values statements, your goals, and the thinking that got you there. That is to be expected, and I encourage you to make note of ideas that strike you as interesting as you read this book. Those notes will help you continue your self-development process on your own. I hope this book guides you to the happy, rewarding, and fulfilling career you deserve.

Part 1
Vision, Goals, Plans

Chapter **1**

Who Are You?

Before setting out on the road to get a job, you should know:

- What job you want

- Why you want it

- How it fits with your overall career plan

To that end, we're going to do some work, collectively labeled *vision*, to identify your personal values, your goals, and the actions necessary to get from wherever you are to where you want to be.

We're going to start with your values!

What are your values?

There are a lot of words to describe the things that are important to us and drive us. People talk about values (as I do here), but they also talk about drivers, goals, imperatives, desires, and more. As I'm going to use words consistently in this book, let's spend a few minutes defining our terms.

A value is a large, driving force in your life. It may drive you in one sector of your life—home, work, spirituality, friends, health—but it is likely that it permeates more than one area. Values wwcan show up in ways that are unique to each of us—and that do not have to make sense to other people!

For example, if one of your values is "helping people" you might spend time doing any of the following:

- Volunteering at your place of worship

- Mentoring junior people in your field

- Mastering the skills to be a great supervisor

- Being a very active parent

- Raising money for a local hospital or charity

People with different values might do the same things . . . but not for the same reasons. Taking the first few items on the list above, a person might respectively be devoted to their religion, enjoy teaching, or be seeking career advancement. That's fine—the point is to know what *your* reasons and motivations are.

In this book, our focus is the values you hold that are front-and-center *as relevant to the world of work*. Some of this will also fall under "likes and preferences," but if we pay attention long enough, we eventually find ourselves led back to values.

Putting your values into words

It may be hard at first for you to put your values into words. You're certainly living your life by your values—whether you know it or not! Because your values are such a motivating and driving force for you personally, they may be somewhat invisible to you. They are the "of course I do things that way" kind of thing.

If you're a very introspective person you may find that this is easier than you think or you may already have a good start on this. If you're not introspective (or if you're new to this kind of activity) it may be taxing.

In both cases, be prepared for your thinking about your values to evolve with time and experience. You may start in one place, and over the next weeks or months different thoughts and realizations will occur to you. That is fine, normal, and expected.

There's no external judgment in your identification of your values. No one is coming to tell you that you are good or bad, worthy or unworthy, whole or broken because of the values you identify. This is an exploration exercise for you.

Let's get into the actual exercise.

Identifying your values

Use *Worksheet 1: What do you value in your workplace?* to help you identify the workplace values most important to you. (For possible updates, go to RylandLeyton.com.)

- Go through the list and identify up to five items that are your own driving forces in your relationship with the world of work.

- Make corrections and edits as needed.

- If you don't see the right thing, write the right thing in one of the blank spaces.

There's no such thing as an all-inclusive list of values! If your value needs to be said in a particular way to feel right and have meaning for you, then write it down in that particular way. There are no wrong answers, only whether what you're saying is accurate or inaccurate as you see it, *for yourself.*

You may want to think of these as "What is important to you at work?" or "What keeps you happy at work?" Right now, we are focusing on your career, not your more global set of values—of which your work is probably one reflection.

If you find yourself unable to narrow down to five or fewer items, then figure out which ones are closely related and ask yourself "What connects these items? What is the essence they are trying to express?" Try to determine the real value you're identifying as something that combines all of the relevant things. It is OK if it seems very large somehow; these should be large concepts—simple concepts—and they may express themselves in a lot of different ways in your mind.

Once you have three to five values identified, move on to the next exercise.

Chapter 2

What Do You Want?

As we are doing career planning, we want to know what we're planning *towards*. There are a lot of options, and again, none are inherently right or wrong; they're just yours. It makes sense for them to be driven by what you like, what you're interested in, and the specific circumstances of your life.

Now let's look at the pyramid diagram, *Worksheet 2: Goals pyramid*.

This diagram is intended to help you put your goals on paper and into a context in which you can give them thought.

Your goals can change, and probably will

If you find you're changing your short- and long-term goals every day, then perhaps your vision of the future isn't clear enough yet to make commitments around—but that's good information to have! It means your activities should focus on determining how to make your vision stable; or, acknowledge that you do not have goals that are consistent over the long term, and you're going to have to build a career that embraces and values *frequent* change!

If you find your vision and goals never change, I'd ask if you have blinders on. Are you examining your experiences? Are you learning and growing? What is keeping you locked into your path?

You could be one of those people who (for example) has known they wanted to be a doctor since they were 10 years old. You went to med school, completed your residency, and qualified for your license, and you've been happy at every step along the way and at every moment with that career ever since you started.

If that describes you—great! But it's not the most common experience, so let's keep an eye out for the alternatives.

Knowing your goals enables spontaneity and opportunity!

I'm about to challenge you to define your goals and make a plan. You need to do that so you have a good perspective on what you want and how you're going to get it.

At the same time, I don't want you to think that you're going to follow the plan perfectly. We just talked about change and how that matters—and now I want to talk about the random opportunities that come up.

The fact is, the universe is better at building interesting things than you are at specifying exactly what will make you happy. On your way through your plan you may find an opportunity presents itself and have one of these reactions:

- Wow! That's a helpful shortcut to my goal, let's try it!

- I didn't know that existed! I would love to do that job—it sounds exciting!

- What a great additional experience to have! I should try that!

Because you're exploring your values and your goals, you will be better positioned to both *see* and *take advantage of* situations that might have otherwise passed you by.

The pyramid diagram

The pyramid diagram has four sections. As you step up the pyramid each section has less room than the one below it. (We'll talk about that more in a minute.)

These sections represent time—starting with "Now," moving to "Next," "Mid-term," and finally "Big Goal."

Both the pyramid analogy and the broad time categories have a specific purpose.

First, all of the things you do for the future are built on the things you do to get there. Obviously, we don't control everything that happens to us. This exercise is about planning and thinking.

Second, it is much easier to plan the things in the time closer to you than the things further out. Don't spend too much time on the furthest things—as they get closer, you can plan them in more detail. You mostly need to figure out things in the first two levels for action—the rest is what you're building towards!

Unless you're already someone who plans their career a lot, you probably haven't thought about it in these four brackets. Here's another way to think about these levels.

Now

The "Now" layer applies to roughly the next year—stuff you're actively doing or plan to do soon. You know exactly what these things are, and you could conceivably start on them immediately.

Examples could include: read a specific book, register for a class, take a web series, start attending professional group meetings, write about a subject that you know well, create a portfolio of your existing work, talk with a colleague, identify a mentor, research schools or education sources.

Generally, these are things you could start doing, and achieve, without undue preparation or work. These are not often things which will meet a goal by themselves, but they build towards one.

Next

Things in the Next section can't be done now, but are less than two years away. This is stuff you know you need to do, but which requires preparation or prerequisites. You may not be able to start on these activities immediately; there may be other people involved or timing that has to be right.

Examples could include: take a class that starts in several months (registering could be a goal for Now), apply to educational programs, get involved in a volunteer group related to your profession, finish a certification, be ready to apply for a specific job (with skills you worked on this year).

Mid-term

Mid-term items are intermediate goals and accomplishments on the path to your successful future. It will take some time and work to get to these, but you can see a path to them. There may be questions to answer, but these are not complete unknowns. These activities are typically in the three- to five-year range.

Examples could include: finish a degree program, earn a promotion, locate a senior-level job with a particular company, have completed writing 36 monthly blog articles, be ready to apply to graduate school, have completed several significant projects in your field. Big Goal

The Big Goal is what everything is building towards. This is the point in your future where you label yourself as having achieved the Big Thing you envision yourself accomplishing. It may be five or more years in the future.

Examples include becoming director, VP, or CEO of a company; earning an advanced degree or license and practicing in your field; being in the top 10% of your field nationally; or similar long-range goals.

Here is an example pyramid showing these time ranges:

Where I am now	Professional bookkeeper
Big Gotal	• Become Sr. Manager of accounting department.
Mid-term goal(s)	• Finish accounting degree. • Get CPA license.
Next	• Apply to 3 accounting programs which prepare me for licensure. • Get agreement from someone to mentor me • Find out what management in the CPA field is like.
Now	• Consider who might be a good mentor. • Interview a CPA to find out if this is really what I want to do. • Identify 3–5 schools and entrance criteria, annual cost, etc. • Research school application deadlines: what is the next deadline and can I make it, or am I looking at the year after? • Identify any qualifying tests, like the SAT. • Decide if I need an exam prep course. • Find out if my employer will help pay for school, or give me schedule flexibility for the program. • Check class options: Full time only? Nights or weekends?

Do the exercise

Using the pyramid diagram—and without worrying too much about drawing inside the lines!—fill in what you can about your long-, mid-, and near-term goals. As with our other exercises, don't worry about getting it "right," "perfect," or "correct." The main thing is to get your thinking on paper so you can examine it outside of your head.

Remember that, as with all of this, this is *just for you.* Be honest, even if you think what you want is unrealistic or that others will not like it. Any given item may or may not involve staying with your current employer—either is fine.

Take 10–15 minutes and write down your vision of your near-, mid-, and long-term goals. Then read the next section and review them.

HINT: This will work better if you don't jump ahead.
Do the exercise now, then read the next section!

Make sure your goals have a lot of freedom!

Much of my career has been spent working with people in the information technology (IT) field. When I have conversations about career goals, people often things like this:

- "I want to be a senior development manager, with a team of about 20 or 30 people."

- "My goal is to be the Chief Technology Officer of a Fortune 500 Company."

- "I'd like to be director of the database group."

- "In the near term, I'd like to be a senior programmer, and we'll see from there."

I think these are fine starting points for a discussion, and I'll guess that some of these goals look like yours—naming a position, title, or job you envision yourself doing. I'd imagine there are feelings of happiness and accomplishment connected to these things, and that's good too.

But I think that this kind of goal doesn't have a huge amount of freedom associated with it. Let me unpack that for you by using an example from my own experience.

Maximizing freedom made the difference

At "the end of the beginning" of my IT career, I was very fortunate. Circumstances had given me several paid months between jobs, so I took a little time to figure out what I wanted to do next. I had been a kind of technology generalist, doing a lot of different things: database programming, web development, business analysis, project management, and people management.

In essence, I was a jack-of-all-trades. I liked it, and my work group loved having me do it, but it wasn't a common job posting. It was more of an accidental thing I'd fallen in to and I couldn't bank on finding it again.

I felt like I would have to choose one of these main areas that made up my previous job if I wanted to advance my career. I wasn't sure which one I wanted to focus on, and I was having problems telling which job postings were interesting to me and which ones weren't.

I realized this was going to be a serious problem when I'd had a few phone interviews where it was hard to show interest and excitement in any opportunity. I was still hoping to find my old job, and that wasn't going to happen.

One day, after an especially difficult phone screen with a recruiter, I realized I was going to have to pick a direction or nobody could help me get the job I wanted. I needed to be able to explain what I wanted to do, but I couldn't figure it out.

So I stopped, took some quiet time (as I've advised you to do), and sat with the problem. And that's when it hit me: all of what I wanted was on a different axis of description from the job title. The title was a helpful label, but it didn't tell the story that I wanted to tell a recruiter or hiring manager.

Here's the job I actually wanted. Given that the compensation was in the range I wanted (figures which were appropriate to the job market and my skills and experiences) the job had to meet all of the following criteria:

- I get to work with people from whom I can learn, and to whom I can contribute.

- I get to work about 50% in my existing skill set, about 25% in my "high-end" skills, and 25% in completely new things. Which skill set is not critical.

- It has to be with a company that I believe I can grow with and stay with for at least three years.

- It has to be with a manager that I think is genuinely interested in the employees they supervise.

This job had no title other than "My Next Job," with the responsibilities and qualifications listed above.

I started applying for positions I thought could meet most of these requirements, which happened to be in project management and business analysis, because that was the skill set I had. I applied full-on for those jobs, showing my qualifications that would enable me to do the job at hand. I left out the rest of my thinking—that I'd be happy with *any* position that met the job description of "My Next Job," in any field.

I had phone and in-person interviews. I withdrew from one or two opportunities where I could tell the manager and I would be a terrible fit. (See "Barb's Rules" in Chapter 13.)

After another month, I was hired by a company I hadn't considered before, in a job I'd never heard of, and which had only been posted to selected recruiters—not through any website!

There were several reasons I got the opportunity to interview in the first place, but one of them was that I told the recruiter what I was looking for. Naturally, I shared my qualifications for the professional fields I was pursuing; however, when she asked "What are you looking for?" I literally told the recruiter exactly the list I shared above. I also told her I was going to take the first job that met my list.

The recruiter knew the hiring manager and felt I'd be a good match because I was passionate about my next job and I was being positive and open about the future. I was the final candidate they could submit.

The manager interviewed me about my skills, personality, interests, and goals. At one point, after we'd established a good rapport and I thought it would be meaningful, I shared my list with her as well.

The distinction? I wasn't just looking for a job I could do. I was looking for something I'd be happy doing, which fit my own goals, and where I could make a difference. I was interested in growing and contributing. That impressed the hiring manager compared to the generic "I can do this job" candidate.

Knowing my values helped me get the job.

OK, Ryland, what's the point?

The point is that by identifying my values, aligning my goals with my values, and making sure I described my goals in a way that gave me the most freedom, I had more choices. I was able to easily filter job postings and interviews to find things that were more exciting! Ultimately, it even helped me stand out from other candidates and get the job.

I could have done any number of the jobs that were posted, but I wasn't satisfied with getting my next J-O-B. I wanted something that fit with my bigger picture, and my bigger picture is to be happy. The things in the description of My Next Job were things that would contribute to me being happy.

It made a difference to me. By defining my goals with greater freedom, I was able to access positions I wouldn't have considered based solely on their job title. I was able to be more spontaneous and flexible about how to achieve my goals.

It made a difference to others. It encouraged other people (in this case, the recruiter and hiring manager) to do the same. They were able to think more broadly about me as a candidate. That enabled them to think about opportunities in which I might be interested that went way beyond the job title on the position and the responsibilities in the description. They had a lot of people with the raw skills to fit the position; this let me stand out!

It will make a difference to you. I want you to have the most freedom to be happy that you can have. That's why I'm encouraging you to revisit your goals and make sure you're defining things in ways that give you the most latitude for success and happiness, and the greatest ability to take advantage of opportunity and spontaneity!

Expanding the freedom in your goals

It can be challenging to rethink your goals in a way that affords freedom and flexibility. The examples in this section should give you some ideas; they illustrate different ways you can think around the traditional titles that you may be focused on when you first start your pyramid.

The bank president

A fictional example I often use to illustrate a goal without much freedom is "I want to be a bank president," where "president" means the person at the top of the organization—the CEO or COO of the bank.

It is a fine goal if that's what you want, but we can unpack it a little to create more freedom in it.

The truth is there are only so many banks, and only so many people who can be presidents of them. It is a very political job, and achieving this kind of goal requires a very long and committed path. The right education, skills, and background—and connections, I expect—are needed.

If this were you, what is it you want out of the goal—what is the motivation for it? Status? Wealth? Power? Authority? Responsibility? Skill? Social regard? Political capital?

Whatever it is, is there a way to get it without fitting it into the very tiny box of a job title?

By finding the reasons for wanting this position, we can hopefully give you more freedom to achieve your own dreams, goals, satisfaction, and happiness.

Saying "I want work that I love doing!" gives us a lot of freedom to figure out what that might look like, and leads us to different questions—and different answers—than just a job title. Even saying "I want prestige" gives us a lot of room. Actors, clergy, elected officials, military personnel, social workers, and tax professionals all can have forms of prestige. Which one appeals to you, and why?

Answering those kinds of questions leaves you with more avenues to your future happiness—and being happy along the way!—than specifying something as narrow as a job title.

The aspiring doctor

I was having a career discussion with a junior colleague of mine, Mike Jamison, who was in his mid-20s and held an early-career position. Mike said right away that he knew his goal: "I want to be a doctor." I was surprised only because our company and our work had nothing to do anything like medicine. He did have a bachelor's degree, but nothing medical related. I asked him if he meant MD or PhD.

"It doesn't matter."

OK, now I was *really* confused. How could that possibly not matter?

"Because I just want to be called Dr. Jamison."

"Mike," I said, "most people who pursue any kind of doctorate—MD or PhD—are really passionate about what they want and why they want it. It is a huge amount of very committed and hard work to achieve either credential. Assuming you could start tomorrow you're looking at a minimum of five years of full-time study to achieve a PhD, and maybe nine years if you go through medical school and residency and so on. What is it about this 'doctor' thing that you're so invested in?"

It turned out that Mike came from a family that had always struggled to make ends meet, as far back as anyone could remember. He was determined to set a new standard for success in his family. He wanted to help others in his extended family and be a name they passed down as "the first one that made it." His BA was a start, but in his mind "Doctor" was an acknowledgment that he'd achieved the highest form of success and would do his family proud.

He hadn't taken the effort into account, and couldn't name a field that he enjoyed enough in to commit to such a course of work—not to say one might not come up in the future! In the meantime, we discovered that this was a driving goal for him. Being seen as successful and "raising up the family" was critically important to him.

When we explored things that connected to this, he was able to identify a few that were more actionable, freeing, and still described what he wanted to do:

- He had to have a career that conferred some prestige or social standing.

- It had to provide enough income for him to help support his own family.

- It had to enable him to contribute to his parents' support in their old age.

- It had to enable him to eventually contribute to charities and his community.

He was willing to put work in to achieve his goals—more education, more experience—and he didn't expect overnight success.

Our plan for him put a lot of those big goals at the top of his pyramid—a position with prestige, at the level of income he wanted.

Figure 4: Mike Jamison's goals pyramid

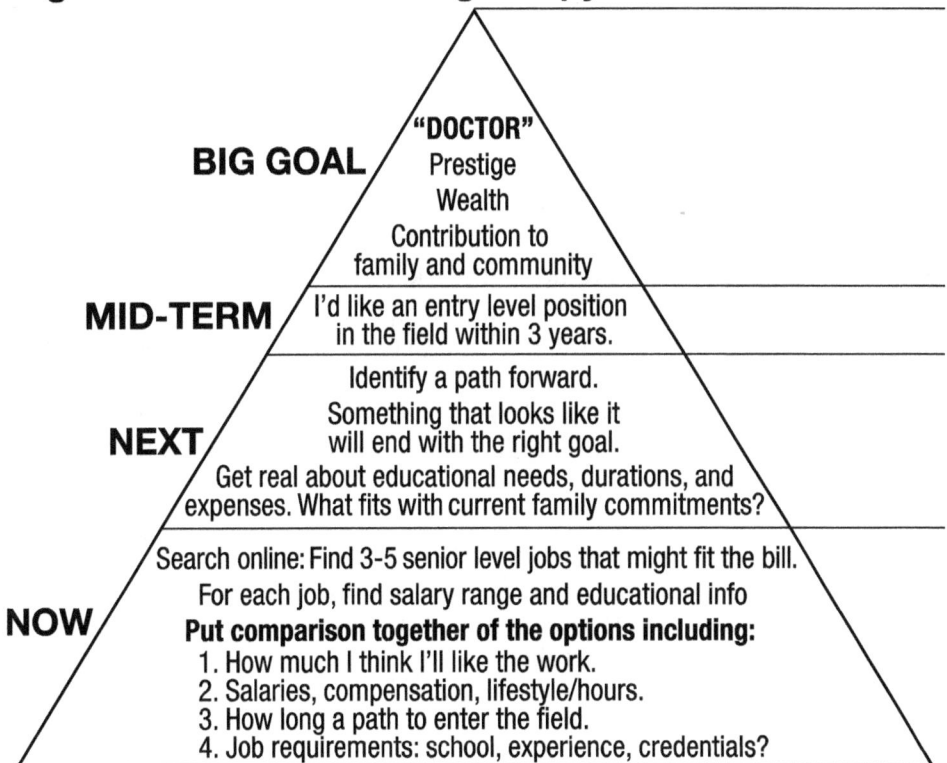

BIG GOAL — "DOCTOR" Prestige / Wealth / Contribution to family and community

MID-TERM — I'd like an entry level position in the field within 3 years.

NEXT — Identify a path forward. Something that looks like it will end with the right goal. Get real about educational needs, durations, and expenses. What fits with current family commitments?

NOW — Search online: Find 3-5 senior level jobs that might fit the bill. For each job, find salary range and educational info. Put comparison together of the options including:
1. How much I think I'll like the work.
2. Salaries, compensation, lifestyle/hours.
3. How long a path to enter the field.
4. Job requirements: school, experience, credentials?

An example of goal setting focused on the need, not the job title.

Now he could gather information to find three to five credentials, professions, and positions that could provide the kind of salary and status he wanted, *and* which seemed like something he'd enjoy working towards and doing. We used that list over the next few sessions to see what direction he was most interested in going to meet his Big Goal.

The environmentalist

At a conference, I was giving a talk on this subject to a group of about 50 people. A young lady had been giving thought to this already.

"I really want to work in something environmentally conscious and help make the world a better place. I'm having some trouble finding a job there which would pay enough to support my family. Everything I'm looking at would require a 30%–50% pay cut from today!"

She liked her profession a lot, and was happy with her job. She felt her company was a good fit for her in terms of the position. Her relationships with her peers and her supervisor were very good. The company, while not environmentally focused, didn't run contrary to her values and was in an industry where she enjoyed the work.

I could understand her concerns.

We talked about creating possibilities: since she felt that this employer was a good fit and she wasn't able to take a pay cut for very good reasons, she could certainly pursue her values outside of work. Pursuing your passion is great when you get to do it at work, but if you can't there are many other opportunities. What's wrong with getting involved with environmental causes on the weekend, or through charitable donations? Park and hiking trail cleanups, river water monitoring groups, regulatory watchdogs, and activist groups can all use additional help. Who knows, something might lead to a job you don't expect—but even if not, you are doing the thing you love doing.

There was no need to constrain her work in this way. Sometimes a job is just a job. You may like it—and I hope you do!—but your passion lives elsewhere. If your work is very stressful, then having engaging activities outside of the office can be a relief.

She decided to keep her job, as it was fine for her and it gave her the resources she and her family needed to have a good life. She found more freedom by looking for a way to pursue her passion outside her job.

By not forcing this important goal and passion into her workplace, she left more room for both of these important things to grow and unfold.

The manager

He said, "I want to be a manager!"

I asked, "Of what?"

"Right now, software development, but later, I don't think it matters."

I was a little confused because his answer was about a subject, and not about people. We talked more, and he clarified this. "I just want to be in charge of people. That always means you're the best at something."

You may be able to tell this was someone young and without a lot of career experience.

We spent some time talking and I discovered a few things:

1. He valued stability, control, and a higher income than he currently had.

2. He saw being a manager as a way to obtain these in his professional life.

3. He had a command-and-control view of leadership, where people would follow him because of his positional authority.

In our conversation I acknowledged what he valued and why, and I understood it from his background. He had gone through a lot of debt, instability, and fear, and even came close to losing his house during a recession. He never wanted to be in that position again, ever. He needed to create a safe and stable base for his career. Income was important to his overall life goals as well.

Placing high value on stability and control is an understandable reaction to those experiences.

I challenged him to explore other ways he could have stability, safety, and income, and to consider what a life in management often means: *less* consistency and control, more being at the beck and call of others. Being in management is typically less stable and controlled than being a non-management employee. The best leaders—*servant leaders*—are more focused on the needs and situations of others than on their own happiness and environment.

Successful modern management isn't focused on barking orders and expecting compliance. It is more about clearing roadblocks, creating environments and companies where others are enabled to make great contributions and are inspired to do so. (See Chapter 18, which discusses careers as an individual contributor versus in management.)

It turns out that this wasn't what he was dying to do. He didn't think he'd like it as a career path. He liked being helpful to others, and liked people in general, but he didn't want to have to be that focused on the needs of others all the time in his work.

After some discussion (and time between talks), he decided that he would create more freedom for himself by having the overall Big Goal of being an in-demand individual contributor. He would keep his skills current and sharp. He would try to become the go-to guy for his specialty at his job, and see how that worked out. Being a helpful expert (as opposed to an unhelpful manager) would probably serve him well with his current employer and if he ever had to look for new work.

His near-term goals became strengthening some specific and valuable technical skills, and thinking about how he could be more helpful to people in his office. He also decided to look for ways to get involved in the occasional request for "special project" volunteers from his team when there was something he felt he could contribute.

He created more freedom by being honest about who he was and what interested him. Not everyone can—or should—manage people. It is genuinely a different skill than "doing a job," and if it's not right for you, there's nothing wrong with that. Admitting it will save you a lot of headaches.

The independent consultant

A friend of mine had asked me to help her think through becoming an independent consultant. She was already a strong professional in the field (accounting), so we talked about her level of comfort with running her own business, finding clients, managing expenses, and the other aspects of being full owner of a company.

"I'm confident I can direct my own work," she said; "the daily tasks of my job, knowing what to do, knowing what the right goals are, and prioritizing to meet the needs of my customer. I like the idea of being more invested in my customer because I have personally arranged the work with them, and giving them what I think is the best service! Some firms I've worked for . . . well, I just don't like the over-and-done way they treat the customer I've served!"

"The problem I have is that I'm not good at selling my services. I'm not good at asking someone to hire me, and I'm not sure how to present myself."

She already knew what she wanted—the Big Goal—but she couldn't see any paths to get there. I challenged her to break it down into smaller pieces and tackle them one at a time. With a little wrangling we got to a list that looked like this:

- I need a way to advertise my services and develop clients.

- I need a way to tell people concisely what I offer.

- I need to become comfortable and confident making the "ask" regarding purchasing my services.

Freedom for her meant developing some skills so she could see what going independent would entail. To be successful she'd need to be comfortable with the business development side of independent work.

In her near term, she decided to take some classes on these skills at a local continuing education program for people starting small businesses and see if that changed her fears at all. She also would talk to other people she knew from a local CPA association who had made this shift and find out what their experience had been.

She created more freedom by getting "unstuck" from thinking and worrying about her roadblocks and taking action to get around them or change her goal.

Chapter 3

Review Your Goals

PLEASE NOTE:
It is best if you have already completed your values list and goals pyramid. If you haven't, I strongly recommend that you pause and do those before proceeding.

Let's review your values and goals for alignment, using some prompted questions and thinking.

As with everything else here, there's not much that can be right or wrong, only what is true for you and not true for you, and what will help you most in pursuit of your goals.

Sit down with these two documents. First, look over your values. Get them concrete in your mind and make sure you can still say "Yes, this represents me well. This is accurate and true about me."

Next look over your goals—including your Big Goal—and consider the following questions about each item.

VALUES

- Is this goal in alignment with my values, or is it against them?

FREEDOM

- Can I state this goal with more freedom from needless constraints like job titles?

- What is the real career value of this goal?

ALIGNMENT

- Does this goal build to something or is it enough by itself?

- If it is building to something, does it make a valuable contribution? Is it essential?

Spend some time looking over the items in your pyramid, exploring your thoughts and feelings about the items there. Feel free to revise, change, and reconsider what you've written. You may do this several times before you decide it represents you. Remember, this is iterative. You are developing a plan, not a locked-in commitment. It should change and grow as you do.

Writing goals that allow a lot of freedom can take time and require a few iterations. You may feel fine with your goals and then something new comes to mind—or you have a new experience—and suddenly you have some new insight. That's OK and part of how it works!

Stop when you think your goal pyramid represents your vision of where you want to be, as well as a reasonably clear and accurate plan of what you will do to get there.

Matching a "freedom" goal to a real job

There aren't a lot of job titles that say, "Be happy doing something you love!" So how do you reconcile your goal with finding a real job for which you can apply?

Those "freedom" goals should be your personal goal. "Work I love doing" is an example. I'm not backing away from that point. It is up to you to figure out what kind of work you love doing, and to achieve that situation. This entire book is focused on successfully exploring, identifying, and achieving that goal.

Along the way you'll have to translate your personal "work you love" into a job description. People will post (hopefully) good descriptions of available positions, and it's up to you to find one that fits the kind of things you love doing. Consider the skills, environments, management style, and other factors that add up to "work you love doing" and look for jobs that have it.

The more freedom in your goals, the more positions you can consider.

Here's another way to think about this. If your goal for TV-shopping is "Sony, 40-inch class, flat-screen," then you'll rule out other things that may meet your real goal: "have a good TV on my living room wall." Other manufacturers, sizes, prices, or products will be visible if you have a broader goal.

The same is true for your career goals.

Expect change over time

There's no reason to try to get this "perfect"—that doesn't exist in this kind of planning. Change is inevitable. The plan and goals need to be "good enough" to guide you and keep you focused on moving in the right direction, as you've defined it.

As I once read somewhere, you may feel strange about changing your goals, or think you somehow "shouldn't." However, think about how things change in your life. Would you let your 15-year-old self make choices about life for your 20-year-old self? How about you at 30 taking advice from a 20-year-old, even if it is you having both parts of the conversation?

You grow, you change, you have new experiences. You learn as you try new things, and this will happen to you as you actively pursue your goals. Expect change to happen, and revisit your goals pyramid from time to time. Apply what you've learned.

Chapter 4

Strengths and Gaps— Getting From Here to There

Now that you have a plan, let's add a refinement step: considering what strengths and gaps will affect how you execute your plan. Are you set up to successfully get to the goal at the top of your pyramid, and the intermediate ones along the way? As with our previous values work, this will help us refine and consider the steps in your plan.

You probably already have an idea of what it will take to get to the kind of position you want to have. By now you know I'm not a fan of labeling your long-term goals with job titles, but this is a case where a sample job posting for the kind of job you want to have will be very helpful.

Let's remember that the purpose of this job posting is to help you find your way to the situation that fits with your goals. We'll talk about a *job* or *position* because the employer is advertising a particular spot in the organization that they need to fill. The flip side of this is that you are trying to locate the position that enables you to pursue your interests and goals. The job posting is where those two intersect.

Note that if you're thinking of working independently as a freelancer or consultant, you will consider who your customers are and what, from a customer point of view, they are looking to "hire." That is the "job" you need to find.

If you already have a clear idea of all the requirements, experiences, skills, and talents you will need to achieve your targeted job, that's great. If not, I suggest going to the online job search board of your choice and printing out a few job descriptions for that kind of position. (This can be a useful reality check even if you think you *do* know what it will take.)

Remember that we are focusing on your career, and that is normally accomplished through a set of job steps. It is fine if those steps (and your plan) change as you grow, learn, and have new experiences.

Our goal at this point is to assess your readiness to get that next position. To do that, let's examine what's on the plus and minus side of your skills versus what the targeted job requires.

Look at *Worksheet 3: Skill self-assessment.* This worksheet is a little less free-form than the others, so let's take a moment to get familiar with it.

Item or Area. On each line, write a skill or accomplishment you think is relevant for your targeted position. You could be looking at your next job, or doing longer-term planning for a future position. It doesn't matter as long as your goal is clear in your mind. Do not go back and forth between the worksheets—pick a goal and work on that one for now.

Be at least moderately specific in this column. See the example page for a few ideas about what this means. The point is that this should clearly line up with something on your sample job description.

Rating. Using a 1–10 scale where 1 is very weak and 10 is exceptional, rate your current ability or accomplishment. Be honest with yourself here. If this is not a total, knock-it-out-of-the-park outstanding accomplishment or strength, don't give it a 10.

You want to consider this from the point of view of a prospective employer: given that the job requires this to be strong, do you meet that need?

You may want to consult with a trusted peer, mentor, manager, or customer of your services about their perceptions of your strengths and gaps. That can be very informative. People often don't know what others see as their strengths and downplay things that are a big deal to the other person.

What does this support? In this column, explain the point of the Item or Area. Does this connect to a necessary core competency? Does it help make your case about something exceptional about you?

You may have rated yourself low or high on this point; connecting it to the overall goal will help you to understand how strong your case is regarding this skill or accomplishment during a job interview.

Needs action? You'll put yes or no here.

Put a YES if either of the following are true:

- This is something you've rated *low* **AND** it is a necessary component of the targeted job.

- This is something you've rated *high* **AND** you have no way to demonstrate to possible employer that it is the strength you say it is.

Put a NO if *any* of the following are true:

- The item isn't relevant for the targeted job.

- You've rated the item in the middle range, but as long as you're not low it isn't going to hold you back from the position.

- This is something you've rated *high* **AND** you *can* demonstrate to a possible employer that it is the strength you say it is.

What are possible next steps that help me meet my goals? In other words, "So, what are you going to do about it?"

Here are some guiding principles to help you think about this for anything where your last answer was "Yes, this needs improvement."

With something you've rated *low* and where this drawback would possibly keep you from getting the position, you need to create a way to gain experience, expertise, and competence in this item. You don't want this to hold you back, and you don't want to be seen as having this kind of gap by a hiring manager!

With something you've rated *high*, you want to make sure you can demonstrate that this is a strength or accomplishment. Pretend you're responding to the following question during an interview: "So you're telling me that (this thing) is a strength for you. What have you done that illustrates this?"

This will help you stand out to a hiring manager. It also gives you something around which to build your career story, a subject we'll cover in Chapter 10.

Your goal when seeking a new position is for the hiring manager not to see any skill gaps, and to see lots of things that make you stand out above the competition.

Stand out to a hiring manager

There are a several ways for a manager to decide who is the "right person" for a position. Here are a few.

One idea of "right fit" is that we are always hired because of our strengths, and not because we have no weaknesses. Those hiring managers are considering how the team fits together, and are invested in creating a team where the various strengths can compensate for others' weaknesses. They see that the *team* has all the capabilities they need—not that every individual has every capability.

Another idea is that a manager is hiring the best individuals that they can hire. In this case, you want to avoid having disqualifying weaknesses while at the same time having strengths that make you stand out—you are something they can't get any other candidate, you aren't the standard "commodity" applicant.

Yet another approach (my own view when hiring) is for the manager to start by describing the ideal candidate for the job, then go through the hiring process. For every position there will be things the manager can teach, things they can't teach, things that any person will have to learn through experience on the job, and things that a candidate absolutely must walk in knowing on day one.

Then, the manager realizes they simply are not going to get a perfect candidate. Each candidate presents about 75% of whatever the manager wishes they could get. This is not because the candidates are defective but because the "ideal" job applicant almost never exists! The manager must evaluate each candidate on their own merits, keeping in mind the set of teachable and must-have-at-start skills, and then decide who will fit the prevailing circumstances the best.

You cannot know which of these types of people is considering you.

In mid-sized to large companies, any decision to make an offer of employment is likely to involve a recruiter, a hiring manager, peer interviews from people already on the team, and a final say from the person above the hiring manager. There may be similar nets and structures if you are looking at much more senior leadership jobs. Each individual will consider your fit for the position from a different point of view.

You need to put your best foot forward. I think that by preparing yourself for the "best individuals" category you prepare yourself for all the others.

By using the self-assessment worksheet and a sample job description and then identifying your strengths to showcase and your weaknesses to remedy, you can create a plan that gets you in position to land the job you want.

Keep your life in balance

Your professional life is just part of your life. At different seasons of your life it may be the primary focus of your time, while at other times it is not as prominent. There's nothing wrong with that.

As they say, nobody ever laid on their deathbed and said, "Gee, I wish I'd spent more time at the office."

Let's assume you've done your self-assessment worksheet and you've put your (updated) goals and activities into your goals pyramid. You've created more freedom in your mid-term and big goals, maybe describing them by attributes rather than job titles, and you've gotten concrete about your action plan in the Now and Next time frames by considering how you'll bring up your weak areas and showcase your strong ones in pursuit of your Big Goal.

I want to encourage you to manage your expectations here. Look at your Now and Next brackets. Are you committing *all* of your free time? If you are doing major independent education, networking, and/or experience growth incremental to your regular work hours, you may find that the time commitment is substantial.

If so, is that wise? Is it realistic? Do you have the support of your family and/or your significant other for the investment of time? Do you have children or others who depend on your availability who will be directly or indirectly affected by your activity?

As much as we are focusing on career now—and I do think that everyone should nurture and develop their career—I encourage you not to sacrifice the other areas of your life in pursuing it. Make sure the other important people in your life are on board with your decisions and can help.

Approach them in a spirit of collaboration and hold their opinions in high regard, especially if they will be affected by or involved with whatever action you're considering. You'll be much happier with the outcomes.

Revisit this from time to time

Remember that this is an iterative process. You'll have your initial plan, and a few months in you'll hopefully have had some new experiences and learning. If those experiences confirm your plan, your goals, and your expectations, that's great! There's nothing wrong with that.

It is also fine if you discover something new and say, "Wow! That goal isn't what I'm interested in at all!" Be grateful! You can make changes to your goals and/or your action plan in light of your new information.

Again: *This is an iterative process. Expect and embrace change.*

Can you imagine how bad it would be to keep following a plan you think is going to get you something you hate? That's the opposite of what we want for you!

Your goals can change. It's very rare that someone starts with goals that are still the same after five years. Opportunities and chance events can lead you to things you never knew about and could not have asked for.

This can happen at any point in life, but is quite common earlier in your career. Don't feel locked into anything just because you decided on it at one point earlier in your life. You may refine the direction you're going—by shifting a few degrees, or by making a radical change!

Part 2
Job Hunting Skills

Chapter 5

The Basic Process of Landing a Job

If you've gone through Part 1, you've identified your values, figured out some goals, and identified gaps.

Now it is time to start talking about how to get that job you want!

This section covers four subjects, in the general order you'll need them:

Resume writing—the approach I recommend for broadest resume reception

Interviewing—the basics and what to expect when you talk with people

STAR answers—the best way to handle most questions at an interview

Career story—a great way to tell an interviewer how you got here and what you're about

First, let's put this in context.

If you are applying for a job, you typically have to pass several stages before an employment offer is made. You need a few tools to get started.

In brief, you'll need a resume, and possibly a portfolio of work samples.

The *resume* will be an easy-to-read, clear, concise summary of your abilities and experiences. I will discuss resumes in detail in Chapter 6.

A *portfolio* of accomplished work is mandatory in some fields, never needed in others, and optional or "nice to have" in other cases. Portfolios are discussed at the end of Chapter 6.

Applying for positions

Let's assume you've sent in a resume, and possibly a portfolio, or otherwise formally applied for the position. Nobody has yet talked to you.

Assuming your resume generates interest, this is typically what's next:

1. Phone screen with either a recruiter or the hiring manager

2. Phone interview with the hiring manager

3. In-person interview with the manager, and probably other relevant people at the office

4. An employment offer

Exceptions to this do happen. For example, if you're applying internally for a position where you already work, you're probably skipping all the phone activities. They'll either interview you or not. If you have done some networking, or you're otherwise already known to the hiring manager in a positive light, they may skip the phone screen. Some companies do more than one in-person interview for critical positions, but this is not common. (At a company of any significant size they'll still need a resume, even if only for legal compliance and documentation reasons.)

Executive interviews—the C-suite and similar—are also different. I expect the career story and STAR answers would be useful there, but you didn't get that interview just because of your resume and a phone screen!

The goal of each step

"Winning" at each step is getting to the next step.

Figure 5: The job hunting model

Typical Model of Hiring Process

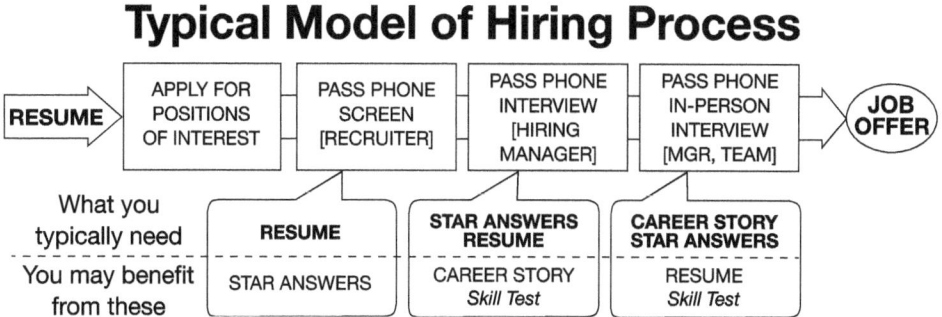

A typical hiring process. Some positions may skip or repeat steps: an internal candidate will probably skip the recruiter phone screen; a critical role may require multiple phone or in-person interviews.

- Your goal with your resume is to talk with a person on the phone.

- Your goal with a phone screen is to meet the basic qualifications and get to talk with the hiring manager.

- Your goal on a phone interview with the hiring manager is to be someone they want for a detailed interview.

- Your goal in person is to show your qualifications, prove your fit with the team, stand out meaningfully from other candidates, and be offered the position.

Chapter **6**

Build a Strong Resume

There are probably as many different opinions about the right resume as there are hiring managers, recruiters, and supervisors. I'm giving you the view from my seat. I think that my approach will help you with all of the situations you may encounter.

Note that recruiters may give you specific instructions when they know the company or manager. I suggest you give them what they request, and help them help you!

The purpose of a resume

Let's be clear about this: the purpose of a resume is to get you to the interview.

Unless you are massively accomplished in your field—you are basically a household name in your profession, everyone knows your work, and the quality of your work is unassailable—your resume by itself will *not* get you a job. (If you're at that level, you probably don't need this book, but if that describes you and you're still reading this, please let me know if you found anything useful!)

As with your interview skills, your STAR answers, and your career story, you should expect to revise your resume a few times.

Here are the basic principles of getting your resume in good shape:

• Keep it professional and to the point.

• Be able to back up what you write down.

• Keep it aligned and relevant to your career story and STAR answers.

Let's review these principles in greater detail.

Be professional and to the point

Spelling counts, even if only to show you took your resume seriously and spent time on it.

Your email address counts. H8RGonnaH8, Linda_Loves_Terriers, and BadBoy1 aren't getting the interview at your typical professional company. Email accounts are easy to get, so get one that is your name or a simple variation. You do *not* want a hiring manager reading it aloud and immediately showing it to a coworker for laughs!

When listing your job history give the company, title, and dates you were employed (month and year). Include a short summary of the work you did as a sentence or two, and a bulleted list of accomplishments. Give more details about recent or relevant jobs and fewer about older and less-relevant jobs.

I advise you to use simple formatting that the eye can scan easily. Hiring managers may read 50 resumes when considering a position, and recruiters may read many times that number. You need to rapidly and easily stand out and convince them it's worth their time to read the resume carefully versus quickly assessing it as "not relevant."

Make no mistake: anyone reading your resume is trying to filter the wheat from the chaff and they will use anything they can to do so!

Use simple experience entries

Here's an example of a good, simple job entry in your resume for a recent and relevant position.

1/2015 to 6/2018

PROJECT MANAGER—Franklin Technologies

Known for successful projects and developing team members.

Responsible for implementation of IT projects from \$2M to \$8M in budget. Managed project through scope, requirements, development, and delivery phases. Responsible for direct supervision of team members, budget accounting, participation with PMO, stakeholders, and technical professionals. Managed projects of increasing complexity and responsibility. Projects typically supported the public-facing website of the company and the customer portal for invoices, payment, project status, and contract review.

- Successfully delivered 8 projects with average budget of $4M, largest $8M.

- Scope of supervision varied from teams of 4 to 50 technical and business professionals.

- Noted as having been in the top 10% of project managers as rated by their teams.

- Commended for successfully handling a major scope change during delivery; accommodated core business needs while keeping to original budget and timeline.

Pretend you are a hiring manager considering someone for a project management position and you see this on someone's resume as their most recent position. You have some idea of what the person did and how good they were at it.

If you were this applicant, you've given the hiring manager several good conversation starters from your accomplishments. You've also given some hooks to your career story. During an interview, this candidate can reasonably say, "I know the core job of a good project manager is to get the job done, I just think that how you do it and the relationships you build along the way are really important. I'm very proud that the teams I work with consider me the PM they'd like to work with again."

Remember: if you don't have any accomplishments in your job, then you should see this as a weakness. Put this on your self-assessment worksheet as something you need to create.

A job entry should show your responsibilities and your accomplishments. What difference did it make that *you* did the job? Why should I consider *you* versus someone else from the stack of 50 resumes that I have? *Worksheet 4: Your resume – professional experience* will help you think through these questions and create an effective resume.

Be visible in applicant tracking systems

Information management systems have made things both easier and more frustrating for job seekers. If you're using any popular job hunting website, you fill out your resume online and you can then submit it easily to any company with a click or two. There's no downside to applying for jobs that look interesting, or that you may only be partially qualified to do. It is just as easy as applying for the one you really want, so why not? Who knows what will happen?

On the flip side, recruiters are getting a ton of resumes from candidates and *must* have a way to quickly determine which should get their attention.

For perspective, a recruiter once told me that in the middle of the Great Recession she had one open position. She received over 500 resumes for it, and only 100 of those people were qualified. While it's not that bad most of the time, even having 50 qualified resumes for one position is a lot.

Applicant tracking systems are here to stay because they make this information flood manageable for the people running the hiring process.

To stand out in these automated systems, you need the right keywords for your field—tools, experiences, skills—listed on your resume.

If you're working with a recruiter, ask them about this. They'll know what works best for you and the job you're hunting. They will know what words are important now and what to possibly avoid. They work with these systems all the time, and they can help you with the ins and outs for your specific situation.

In technical fields, a list of methodologies, tools, and software with which you are experienced is part of the resume. This can be a simple, even lengthy list at the end of your resume. You should also list the most important relevant keywords as part of the appropriate job entry.

In my own case, I like to ensure that any keywords or buzzwords I think are relevant or "hot" right now fit into a job entry as noted above. I make them part of a solid sentence about something I have done. Using our previous project manager example, I might add this line to an experience block: "Drove transparency, collaboration, and communication through expert use of Microsoft Project, Slack, Jive, and Asana." (These are all software tools commonly used in that field.)

Alternatively, put a short list of the most common tools you need as part of your professional experiences. Keeping with the project manager example, adding this sentence to the summary of professional experiences would possibly work: "Expert user of Microsoft Project, Slack, Jive, and Asana."

If the job posting requires specific skills or abilities, make sure they are clearly stated and easy to find on the resume. Put them early in a sentence, next to a bullet point. Don't make the reader hunt for it in 8-point type somewhere in the middle of a paragraph.

The search system will bring up your resume as a match no matter where the word is, but you want the human who then examines it to not think of this as "just an added keyword." You want it to be clear that it is relevant and possibly even core to your abilities.

Remember, at this stage we are just trying to stand out from the rest of the people enough to get the phone screen.

Checklist of resume sections

Here is a simple checklist to help you construct a simple, professional resume without pulling your hair out:

1. Contact information

2. Theme or positioning statement

3. Summary of professional experiences

4. Short list of core skills, experiences, and competencies

5. Experience

6. Education & credentials

Remember, everything you include on your resume should fit somehow with your career story. This may take time to refine. Don't hold up a resume if you have to provide one, just always consider it a "living document" until you land a job you want to have!

Theme or positioning statement

Start by giving the reader a framing idea of who you are in a theme or positioning statement. This is *one or two sentences* that invite them to begin to understand you. It is not a long run-on sentence using 10 commas.

Here are a few examples:

Our example project manager:

An experienced, skilled Project Management Professional (PMP) focused on business success and project teamwork, seeking a company with similar values.

A new graduate:

A software engineer looking for a position with a company where I can make a difference, bringing my new skills to the workplace. I stay current on what's new and what's next!

An experienced manager:

A team manager who focuses on taking new talent and making them your lifelong employees, I strive to create the next generation of your company.

Pretend you are the manager reading these statements. Each gives you some idea of the career story of the candidate. If that story sparks interest, you'll probably at least ask the person for a short phone screen. For any job seeker, that's a win.

Remember: winning at this stage means getting a call to interview, not getting a job offer.

Summary of professional experiences

Your summary of professional experiences can be two or three sentences which support your theme. It can be experiences, skills, or accomplishments. It should stand out and grab attention, so make sure it is relevant.

Here are some examples, following on from our statements above.

An experienced, skilled, Project Management Professional (PMP) focused on business success and project teamwork, seeking a company with similar values.

- 8 years' PM experience; largest project was $16M, 3 years, and a team of 60 people.
- Recognized for being the successful PM that clients and team members want again.
- Practices servant leadership with teams and business value with clients.

A software engineer looking for a position with a company where I can make a difference, bringing my new skills to the workplace. I stay current on what's new and what's next!

- Graduated [last year] with a 3.8 GPA, MS in Software Engineering.
- Participated in three internship projects with Fortune 500 companies. (References available.)
- Excited about and experienced with cloud computing, open source, and mobile development.

A team manager who focuses on taking new talent and making them your lifelong employees, I strive to create the next generation of your company.

- 20 years in the workforce, 15 of them in management. Teams from 5 to 25 direct reports.
- Known as "the new guy manager," taking new talent and turning them into top talent.
- Focused on employee development and progress.

I would suggest three to five bullet points. More than that and you will risk losing the focus of the reader. You want something the eye can scan quickly and the mind can absorb easily.

Again, your goal is to hit the key points about your career story and make the hiring manager actively curious about you. If you succeed, they'll look for more on your resume to fill in details; if they see further skills and abilities which interest them, they'll arrange to speak with you.

Core skills, experiences, and competencies

Your core skills, experiences, and competencies can be provided in a short list relevant to your industry. It will probably have items very specific to your field which are relevant for a hiring manager (or recruiter) to see. This is less about accomplishments and more about the activities and skills needed for the job you're seeking.

Here are a few examples, attempting to select very broad choices for illustration.

Management: Recruitment, selection, and hiring of candidates; performance management; annual evaluation, awarding salary changes and bonuses, terminations, and discipline.

Visual merchandising: Selection of inventory for display, creation of displays, training other team members, participation in merchandising team recommendations.

Project management: Budget management, team selection, stakeholder management, project reporting, audit compliance.

Car salesperson: Customer relationship management, inventory knowledge, understanding of finance options, levels and types of sales success achieved.

I suggest using no more than three to five lines for this. You can use multiple columns on the resume to fit this in, as typically these are short statements.

Experience

This is what you've been wanting them to read. Use the simple experience entry format I recommended early in this chapter. This portion of your resume can run up to two pages. More than that, and you're either talking too much about one or more positions or talking about too many positions.

Make sure you include the positions that are relevant to your career story, as long as they're not ancient history. That seminal experience 20 years ago doesn't need to be on your resume; it is part of the conversation at the interview. Where necessary for very old positions that show a history of consistency, use the dates you worked there, company name, job title, and a one- or two-sentence summary of the job.

Education & credentials

If you are recently out of school, or your educational credentials matter for some reason, then you may spend more time on this section. Otherwise, this is a simple list of facts. If it was 15 years ago, being a high school chess champion or having a 4.0 GPA doesn't matter anymore. You've had jobs since then; explain what those jobs contributed to your professional development and the work you want to do at this point in your career.

If you have any relevant professional certifications or licenses, you should certainly include those. Include necessary information for credentials you list—and assume people will verify these if they are critical for the position.

. . . And maybe your hobbies, interests, and activities

I'm not a big fan of hobbies and interests on the resume. On the one hand, listing these can invite someone to consider you a little more as a well-rounded person. Your participation in sports, community involvement, and hobbies are all neutral topics that can do this. If you have room and want to include these things, I'd call that "flavor."

I would not include things that reveal your race, religion, controversial political views, or membership in a legally protected class. You do not know who is reviewing the resume. And no matter what, those topics should not be relevant to the hiring decision.

If something about a hobby or interest is relevant to your candidacy for a position, that is a different story. Treat that like any other job entry on your resume. Here are a few examples:

> You are looking at a sales position, and you raised $50,000 last year to build a Little League stadium in your community. You can show transferable skills based on your fundraising.

> You are trying to make the case for your leadership, judgment, and management skills. You've been the president of your 200-unit condominium association for 10 years running, having won re-election four times. You can show cases where you've had to handle large-scale

renovations, build agreement around budget items, and handle issues between the management company and owners.

You are applying to join the IT department of a car dealership, and you have restored and rebuilt several classic cars. You have relevant knowledge about cars, the car industry, and automotive maintenance. This will help you with customers and employees.

These kinds of hobbies can make a difference! A friend of mine got his first job out of college because of a hobby. The hiring manager had told their HR person, "I'm tired of you bringing me people who can only do one thing at a time! I need someone who can really juggle things and get them done!" My friend was a part-time professional juggler—bowling pins, rings, torches, even juggling on a unicycle. He got the interview and got the job. I would love to have heard the management side of that conversation!

Experience counts
much more than aspirations

If you are a mid-career or experienced professional, you have a record to stand on. People expect to see what you've done, not what you promise you can do. They'll use your history to decide if you can do the job that's on the table. You need to have a career story about your journey with which they can connect.

If you are a new professional—just out of school, a career changer, or similar—then your story is more one of preparation and readiness for the opportunity. You bring something to the table in terms of just-learned, new, or cutting-edge skills. If you are a career changer, your experiences or transferable skills may be important.

What about cover letters?

As with resume formats, you will get a lot of different opinions about cover letters. An internet search on this will produce conflicting opinions and professional advice in the first page of results!

I personally am not a fan of cover letters. I think they're a waste of time and that nobody will read them.

This is why:

- Everyone sounds wonderful in a cover letter. It is a press release you write about yourself, not a news article researched and written by a third party.

- They have no set structure, so as an interviewer it is hard to get anything useful out of one.

- They are a huge opportunity to make a bad impression on the reader for reasons you will never know, and about which you will get no feedback.

- Your writing is on display. This may or may not be a core competency in your field. This carries lots of risk for real no reward.

So, I do not offer a cover letter by default.

If you are *required* to write one for a position, here is my limited advice:

- Keep it short. More is not necessarily better.

- Don't say anything you can't support with your resume.

- Organize your information very clearly. Assume the reader may be skimming the page.

- If you are working with a recruiter for this position, make sure they read the letter before it is submitted. There is probably a reason they want it.

There is one situation where I certainly would prepare a cover letter: you are changing careers and you want to explain how your past prepares you for the new career. You can show how the skills necessary for the future have been earned in your past, as well as how they will transfer and be relevant. I recommend showing the letter to colleagues and recruiters in your targeted field and taking their feedback seriously.

Again, your goal is to get the interview. This kind of cover letter can help you overcome the problem of the hiring manager not seeing directly relevant experience on your resume. It can also help you be a standout candidate—you aren't what they see every day!

Do I need a portfolio or work samples?

If you are in a field that has a significant "design" aspect of any kind—such as graphic design, user experience, visual merchandising, architecture, or engineering—you will need a portfolio. Fields like software engineering are starting to expect work samples as well.

In my own work, which has involved a lot of technical or informational writing, portfolios are usually optional. Having samples has been helpful—in one case being a deciding factor in getting the position. In other cases, I offered them and they were declined.

Some people's work is public: window designs, print or media advertising, public-facing websites, and so on. They can take an image of the work product, write an explanation of their contribution, and use it at an interview. Because the end product is public, there's no issue here. (If the end product was never released, that's a different story, and it might or might not require permission.)

A common complaint among job seekers is, "I can't use anything from work—it's all proprietary and I can't show it outside the company!" If that's true, definitely do not display anything labeled proprietary to a prospective employer unless you have *written* permission! The interviewer might (correctly) get the impression that you don't know how to appropriately handle company information.

Instead, create relevant samples for fictional assignments based on assignments you've had, or skills you want to display. You can use these samples for anything. Yes, they are fictional, but treat them as though they were real-world assignments and make them representative of your best work. I suggest having a colleague in your field critique them before you show them more broadly.

You may also want to create a separate catalog of your projects. You don't have enough room to list every project you ever did on your resume; you need to synthesize and highlight the key points, not every detail of every project or task. But you can typically submit more than one document, so a catalog can help you display the breadth or depth of your experience. While this is not part of your resume it still makes an important contribution. You can reference the list from your resume.

I suggest a table format that a reader can easily scan. Here are some examples for your consideration. Think about how these could apply to your own situation and create one that represents you well.

Software developer

List the software projects you worked on; the tools, languages, and applications you used and how you used them; technical or other problems you solved; the nature of the customer; and your specific contribution to the project.

Construction project manager

List each project or company name, location, the kind of construction you oversaw (steel, plumbing, electrical, etc.), your scope of responsibility, budget or staff levels, challenges you overcame, and project outcomes.

Visual merchandiser

List each company, the location, whether it was an interior or window display, size of space, kinds of merchandise, goals of the display, the target audience, and the results of your work.

Graphic designer

List the types of campaigns or products you handled, media (print, video, web), effect of your work product (lift in sales, engagement, opinion), challenges you overcame, and any measures of your work compared to historical work by others.

If you can, supply the following for each entry:

- A link to a positive public review or image of the work product

- Any awards or commendations for the project or your contribution

- Any concrete, material, measurable benefit or improvement that the project provided

Should I customize my resume for every position?

Unfortunately, the answer is, "It depends."

If the position is fundamentally the same and your resume will be good, then no. I would still check for relevant keywords, and possibly highlight different experiences in your portfolio that are relevant to the specific opportunity. If you're using a cover letter, make appropriate changes to it as well.

If the positions are radically different—different qualifications, different relevant experiences and so on—then yes you need to make edits and fit the job description. In this case, I'd guess you are someone who can apply for jobs in a variety of fields and need to make your case correctly for each one. You should have a resume for each job category and tweak those as needed for each opportunity. If you're completely revising your resume for every position, I think you've gone way past the point of diminishing returns. You don't know enough about the reader to customize things that strongly. Make your best written proposal, and stop.

Chapter **7**

Rock the Interview

If things go as you want, you are going to have several conversations, probably with different people, regarding your qualifications for the job.

Typically, these will include:

- A brief phone screen with a recruiter

- An initial telephone interview with the hiring manager

- An in-person interview with the hiring manager, someone on the team, or a panel of interviewers

You must take each one seriously. I'm a fan of thinking that the interview process begins when you start traveling to the meeting. If it's a phone interview, pretend you're starting about 15 minutes early, to get your mind and body settled in a quiet and controlled space to have the call. Shift into your work persona. Think about your qualifications, refresh your memory regarding your prepared answers and the points you want to make in the interview.

You need to be ready for any "brief" call to turn into a full interview. Be glad if it does—it indicates interest and investment on the part of the interviewer!

My experience is with professional positions in office settings. If you are doing something else—such as forestry, construction, police work, or a field based more in physical skills—you may need to modify this advice for your situation.

You have a lot of goals in an interview. You know this and your interviewer knows this. How well you handle all of those goals is part of what they will assess.

Let's remember that your interviewer has a lot going on in the interview as well:

- They have to find the right person for this position.

- They may be trying to judge how each candidate will add to the team already in place, or offload work from people overloaded by missing team members.

- The interviewer is *definitely* being judged on the quality of candidate they present to, or hire for, the company. A manager who consistently hires "problem" employees is failing at an important part of their job.

Basic interview preparation

This informal checklist will help you prepare for any interview, by phone or in person.

- Arrive, or settle down, at least 15 minutes early.

- Take a deep breath, and settle into your "work mindset." Give the up-coming interview your full attention. The rest of your day will wait.

- Review your resume.

- Review or write down the points about your experience and qualifications that you want to make during the interview.

- Have a few questions to ask the interviewer. Preferably, these should show interest in the job or company and be relevant to the position at hand.

   Relax. Confidence helps!

Interview formats

Companies and managers have several ways they can interview you. They will commonly use more than one approach before making an offer, and these approaches may come from different people. Here is a little about each type of interview and a few tips on what to do in these circumstances.

Social interviewing

The social interviewer works quickly to set you at ease, gain your confidence, and have a "simple chat" with you. Questions typically revolve around your hobbies and interests, possibly your family, and do not appear directed strongly at work subjects.

Some of this is normal in an interview to establish rapport and set a candidate at ease. Knowing if a candidate has basic office social skills is part of an interview.

But if it never shifts from here, you may be dealing with a social interviewer.

The social interviewer is trying to make a gut-feeling decision about how well you will fit with the team. There's not much you can do here except try to make a positive impression. Be genuine, but stay within professional boundaries.

Never discuss or joke about politics, religion, drugs, or sex, even if the interviewer does. If they are talking about any of these subjects, it is either a trap *or* they are trying to find out information that shouldn't be relevant to the job *or* they don't know what they're doing in the interview.

The information you disclose about yourself should be real and business appropriate, and you should have some things picked before the interview. Have some innocuous facts about your favorite hobbies, sports, books, or movies ready so you can make small talk. Avoid controversial, divisive, or heated topics, including news.

Every interviewer is looking to make sure you fit socially—that is, you're not picking your nose at the interview, you're dressed appropriately, you can carry on a conversation to the degree they feel is a minimum, and so on. You always have to pass this test, for any job.

The difference is that the social interviewer is going to rely completely on how much they *like you* as they consider you for the job. Your qualifications may not matter very much.

Skills-based interviewing

For technical or professional positions, a team member will often meet with you and run you through a sample set of problems that only someone with the right skills can solve. This helps weed out people who hope to fake their way to a position or who are seriously "puffing" their resume.

Skills interviewing is a norm in technical positions today. You will probably be told to expect a skills test of some kind if you will be participating in one. It could be a group problem-solving situation where you work with others, or it could be completely solitary. Either of these could take from 30 minutes to a couple of hours, depending on the nature of the assessment and the company culture.

Either way, this is generally a good thing. You get to show your skills in an unbiased way to people of similar skill sets. They can appraise your abilities instead of having to trust what you have said. At the end, both they and you will know if you have the necessary skills to be successful in the position.

In a group situation, you'll be able to assess how much you like working with this team of people—and they're definitely doing the same with you! I suggest you emphasize your ability to listen to others, give concise and clear answers, make a contribution, and collaborate well.

Behavioral interviewing

Behavioral interviews are also the norm in hiring practices today. This is so common people may not know they're using this practice!

For positions where skills can be objectively assessed, your interview may have both a skill test and a behavioral portion.

The goal of a behavioral interview is to find out how you might handle different situations that can occur in the real world and which require judgment. The interviewer may present you with cases of competing goals or priorities, or with situations that assess how you manage conflict, how you handle stress, or possibly how you deal with pressure from coworkers or customers.

The behavioral interviewer will ask questions that are relevant to the position. The answer format is open-ended, free-form, and tells a lot about a candidate. The interviewer wants a direct, unambiguous, concise answer that addresses their point. This is not always easy. You can ask for some clarification, but it may be limited—this is intentional.

Behavioral interviews may include questions like these:

- Tell me about a time you had to resolve a conflict with a coworker.

- Tell me about a time you failed at something, and what you did about it.

- Describe the environment in which you do your best work.

- How do you manage your time during your work day?

- Give me an example of a time when you worked as part of a team to jointly solve a problem.

- What was the best day you've ever had at work, and why?

Interviews for positions that use management or supervisory skills can also include questions like these:

- Give me an example of a time you had to help a struggling employee.

- How do you motivate your team?

- As a manager, how have you handled having to implement a company directive that you didn't agree with?

- What do you do to reward success?

- Tell me about the best and worst annual review you've ever had to give to someone.

The bad news is that these are just samples—the list is endless! Do an internet search for "behavioral interviewing" and you'll find tons of sample lists.

Be glad if you have a behavioral interviewer. They know what information they're looking for, and if you can help them find it you have a good chance of standing out from other candidates in a positive way. You're going to use STAR answers to do this, and we'll get to that in Chapter 9.

Disorganized interviewing

Not every company trains or prepares their hiring managers to do interviews, so some people are just winging it. It is also possible that the interviewer is a last-minute substitute, or that the time they were going to use for preparation had to be spent on something urgent. There are many similar, understandable reasons for an interviewer to appear disorganized when they walk in the room.

In any case, your task is the same: help the person find the information you think they most want to have, and make a good impression while doing it. Helping them to the right information is a good thing and will help you stand out.

Do not take someone who presents as disorganized as a waste of your time or think they are foolish. They may simply be getting ready to get down to the good questions and need a few moments to organize their thoughts. Interviews happen in the real world with real people. The interviewer could be buying a few moments with a broad question while they quickly scan your resume for things that are interesting to them and transition to behavioral interviewing.

You'll know you're dealing with a disorganized interviewer if they stay with big, nebulous questions and never get to anything directly related to your qualifications, skills, experiences, or behavioral answers.

A disorganized interviewer will often start with questions like these:

- So, tell me about yourself.

- What are your qualifications for this job?

- How did you hear about us?

- What do you know about me?

- What do you know about our company?

Most interviewers will shift from these to something more targeted and behavioral, and you should shift with them.

A word of caution about this: Sometimes these are perfectly good questions. You should be prepared for several of these; it shows background research and interest on your part. Let's review some possible questions and answers.

"What do you know about me?" If you're interviewing with someone who is very demanding, in a unique position, or well known in the field, and/or if something about them personally is very relevant to the job, then don't assume they're disorganized. Alternatively, if you and they basically know that you have the right skills for the job this could just be a social interview in disguise to see if you will fit in with the existing team.

"Tell me about yourself." This is a good time to tell your career story.

"What are your qualifications for this job?" Have three or four bullet points ready as to why you fit this job. Be prepared to go to your career story or STAR answers, depending on what the interviewer does next.

"What do you know about our company?" This is a good opportunity to share any industry knowledge you have about the company, gross revenues, major products or initiatives you're aware of, and so on. You can show background preparation here and this is important to some hiring managers.

Interviewing over a meal

Remember, until you have started the job you are still interviewing for it 100% of the time. There are no breaks, there is no downtime. You are center stage every minute.

If you are asked to have a meal or a drink with the interviewer or your prospective work group, planned or unplanned, you are still being interviewed. There are many good reasons for such an invitation, including wanting to see if you still appear to be the same person they've been interacting with when you're not in a formal setting, or investigating if you show appropriate self-control when around alcohol.

The reasons are endless, but your reaction should be the same: treat this as a continuation of the interview. Discuss appropriate social topics, do not attempt to keep things 100% on work subjects. Be yourself, but remember that you're at a (potential) workplace, not in a social setting.

Safe topics for this situation are hobbies, sports, professional interests, and so on. Do not get into politics or current news if you can avoid it. Never make jokes about or discuss sex, drugs, or religion.

This is a good opportunity for you to ask the interviewer or team questions that show your interest, and invite them to disclose things as well:

* What have you done lately that is challenging?

* When is the last time you were out as a team?

* What do you like about working here?

The people you are with have a lot of room to be open in this situation, and they'll likely do just that. You should have some things you'd like to know about! This shows interest in the team and the position, as well as supplying good information that you should want to have.

Chapter 8

Avoid Legal Landmines

This is a hard topic about which to give you advice, and I must first say that I am not a lawyer and I am not giving you legal advice. The following is conventional—not legal—advice, and is based on purely my own experience as a person who works in the United States. If you run into one of the following issues or think you have been discriminated against, please consult an attorney.

Things vary widely, and the boundaries around what is and is not acceptable to discuss are always evolving. I'm trying to give you the opportunity to consider difficult questions in advance. How you handle them is up to you.

In the United States in 2019, it is unlawful for an interviewer to ask you about certain subjects. In addition, certain groups of people are explicitly protected against discriminatory practices during hiring; these groups are known as *protected classes*. Protected classes are defined at the federal, state, and sometimes local levels, and may vary in certain jurisdictions, but they typically include race, color, religion or creed, national origin, age, gender, veteran status, family status, and disability. Some jurisdictions include sexual orientation.

You may be asked to fill out a form requesting information about your membership in a protected class when you submit your application. These forms are used for compliance reasons and are supposed to be stored separately and not given to the interviewer. That's fine, normal, and expected.

Regarding your resume

For most jobs in the U.S., some things should not be included on your resume. In other countries or in special cases, these concerns may not apply to you.

Your resume should not disclose your family status (married, single, divorced, whether or not you have children), nation of origin, age, race, ethnicity, or religion.

During an interview

If an interviewer asks about any protected class subject, they have probably crossed a line they are not supposed to cross. However, some people will do this without knowing they have done so or without intending any harm. They may simply be trying to get to know you, and not use the information to your detriment.

Only you can decide what to do when an out-of-bounds question comes up.

Here are a few examples. They could be meaningful, or meaningless. You cannot know.

- I have two kids myself. How about you?

- There are a lot of Greek folks here. Will you fit in?

- Our work hours are very strict. With your kids, will that be a problem for you?

- You may become one of the first Latin employees our company has hired. Do you think that will be a challenge for you?

You have a few ways to handle a question like this.

Answer it. Nothing prevents you from answering an inappropriate question. This may be a good option for you, as it gets your reality on the table. If there's a problem there, you may be weeding out a workplace that wouldn't be a good fit for you down the road. This is not for everyone.

Deflect it. Instead of answering, you may prefer to deflect to another subject or provide a neutral answer that gives no information. If the interviewer asks how many kids you have, you might reply "Thank you for asking! My family is fine with this opportunity." Or if they ask about your ethnic background, you could say, "I'm glad this place embraces diversity so readily!" It is possible that this will be noticed, but a sensible interviewer will not pry, possibly realizing they're out of bounds.

Point it out, possibly with humor. An interesting option, especially if you're applying for a management position, is to say something along the lines of "I like how you did that! Very clever of you. Yes, as a potential manager, I am able to identify questions that could get us in trouble during an interview. Thank you for checking on that." The interviewer may have any number of reactions, and I cannot say this will help you get the job. However, they put you in this position. You have to deal with it, intentional or not.

Volunteering information

If you volunteer information about belonging to any protected class, that is your business. They're still not supposed to base a hiring decision on it, but the information is there now, where otherwise it might not have been.

Nothing prevents you from volunteering information. The following are examples where a person might do this for very good reasons.

- "My spouse and I make sure that one of us is there to greet our kids when they get home from school. As long as I plan it ahead, mark my calendar, and handle any responsibilities, can I expect this level of schedule flexibility?"

- "I am very active in our Latin American Employee affinity group in my current job. Do you have different affinity groups at this company, and if so, what kind of contributions do they make?"

The better employers out there do understand that people juggle home and work commitments and that this is a common skill now. They appreciate diversity in people, thoughts, and abilities.

Unfortunately, not everyone is a "better employer." You should consider where you stand on this before such a situation arises for you.

Chapter **9**

Light the Way
With STAR Answers

Interviewers want to know more about you than what is on your resume. The best way to give them that, no matter what kind of interviewer you encounter, is a STAR answer.

What is a STAR?

STAR is a very common acronym used in hiring and recruiting practices. It stands for:

Situation   What was happening? What was the context?

Task   What was the task/outcome that needed to be accomplished?

Action   What did you do?

Result   What was the actual outcome?
                  What is the result? The "So what?" of the story.

The idea is to give a concise and well-formed answer to interview questions. *Worksheet 5: STAR answers* will help you create STAR answers to highlight your skills and value to the interviewer. Some examples are at the end of this chapter.

How to use a STAR

Whenever you are asked a question in an interview, your goal is to leave the interviewer with no question that you have the right skills and abilities for the job. STAR lets you do that concisely.

Behavioral interviewers are often trained to look for STAR answers and to ask questions that elicit them.

You should rehearse three to five STAR answers that showcase your strengths and present you in the best light for the job. Use your completed self-assessment worksheet to develop these answers.

It is *very unlikely* that your prepared answers will match up with exactly what the interviewer asks. However, practice will enable you to use the right pieces at the right time or improvise a sensible and informative answer at need.

Let's say you have listed one of your strengths as solving problems between departments with different responsibilities. You might rehearse the STAR answer below in case an interviewer says, "Please give me an example of a time when you had to solve an interdepartmental problem."

(S) Often in my work, I'm the person my boss asks to resolve service-level problems with our warehouse. We are a young company and we are still shaking out the processes between our order team—where I work—and our fulfillment team, who handles picking orders from the warehouse and shipping them out.

(T) We were having a problem with our priority orders. Customers were paying for "priority shipping & handling," but the company wasn't meeting the two-day limit for these orders to ship from the warehouse. Since we pride ourselves on customer service, this was a problem. My manager asked me to solve it.

(A) I put together a one-hour meeting with a manager and one of the warehouse employees who handles picking and shipping orders, as well as myself and another order clerk. I prepared a brief problem statement and agenda for the meeting. I focused us on the problem and not on finger-pointing or blame, which did crop up a time or two. When it did, I redirected to the problem by pointing out we're all one team, working on one issue together.

Together, we worked through a few orders where problems had come up and caused delays. We identified both communications and process problems between our groups that we could solve. We identified the ones we could change quickly, and which ones we'd try later if that didn't fix things.

(R) It took about two weeks to get the changes fully implemented in our departments, but problems related to priority orders were cut by 75% over the next month, and customer emails about this problem became very rare.

Verbally, that will take about two minutes. It is a good, short answer that gives the interviewer a lot of information. They can ask for details—or you can insert them, if it's relevant to their question—about exactly what kinds of process improvements were made.

You can use this same STAR answer for several things:

- To support your resume point about being a problem solver

- To make a point about being able to make and execute a plan

- To show that you can be given a goal and independently figure out how to achieve it

- To show how you can manage others through a change

- To show how you can talk about problems without finger-pointing and blaming

- To show how you have learned the value of teamwork and collaboration

A good STAR answer will align with your career story. (See Chapter 10 for more on career stories.)

STAR examples

"Tell me about a time you had to resolve a conflict with a coworker."

Situation. Jennifer and I were peers on a team, in different functional areas. She had come up through the company and had a very specific way of doing work that she expected me to adopt as well. I was new and had been told by our manager that it was fine to come up with new ways to do things as long as the result was good—innovation might help us as long as we got the job done! Jennifer didn't like my work style, but our manager was fine with it, it worked for me, and my service to our customers was considered very good, so it wasn't an issue.

Task. After I had worked there about two years our manager was promoted to director, and Jennifer became the new team manager, including over me. She imposed expectations on me to do work the way she wanted it done, which would make my work less efficient for me and less timely for customers *but* more understandable and predictable for her, given her background.

Action. After butting heads several times and being told by her that I just had to take her instructions, I was able to get her to talk with me in a no-expectations conversation. I told her I understood that she would like my work products to be reliable and predictable, and I wanted to make sure she felt supported as the team manager. We were able to create working agreements about checkpoints in assignments that would give her more security about how work was progressing, while maintaining my overall efficient work pattern.

Result. We had to adjust things once or twice, but this actually brought Jennifer and me together as a more effective team. She came to understand more about my work tasks and why they were handled differently. This understanding helped her interact with other groups in the company. I also came to value and appreciate her experience and history with this employer. Both of these things would come up as positives over the next few years as we worked together.

"Tell me about a time you failed at something, and what you did about it?"

Situation. There was one time when I was writing software requirements for a project. I had a particularly important fact written down completely wrong, and it led to about 25% of my 150 requirements being in error. The project couldn't start with that many corrections to make.

Task. This was discovered in the middle of a requirements review and approval meeting with roughly a dozen developers and business stakeholders. I was very frustrated and embarrassed. My credibility was on the line! I had to do something to keep the project on track, protect quality, and avoid causing a delay.

Action. I paused the review for a moment and asked the team for agreement about how to handle this. A lot of the work was still valid, I just couldn't be sure exactly which items might need correction in this specific moment.

I proposed that we keep doing the review and if an item might be affected by my error we would just identify it and move on to approving the next unaffected one. This meeting was on Thursday, and I would make all the necessary corrections by the next Monday morning and email the updates out, asking the group to review and approve only those items by Wednesday. Then I could correct any still-remaining errors or edits, and we could start the project on time the week afterwards.

The team agreed to my plan.

Result. The meeting went a bit slower than we expected, but we did get through everything. We had about 35 items that needed examination and correction in some way, and I did more analysis and writing on Friday and over the weekend. I met the Monday morning deadline the team had agreed to. It was a rough weekend, but it was the right thing to do. The team appreciated my extra effort.

We got approvals and made a few more edits that week, and we started on time.

"Give me an example of a time you had to help a struggling employee."

Situation. I was supervising a team and there was one person, Dave, who did good, solid, consistently reliable work. Dave also had a really hard time with the people side of things. He thought of himself as helpful, but other employees—both in and out of my group—frequently considered him hard to work with. He was rigid about time schedules and often gave off an attitude of superiority. In some cases he could be defensive.

At the same time, Dave wanted to be assigned to more difficult projects and be considered for a promotion. I couldn't get either of those things done unless his behavior changed.

Task. To best serve Dave and the company, I would have to get Dave to understand what part of his own behavior was holding him back from what he wanted to achieve. I had to get his willingness to change and set him up for success.

Action. I set up a meeting with him on a Friday and let him know I just had some concerns to discuss with him. I made sure he understood this wasn't a disciplinary meeting in any way and he was still coming to work the next Monday.

At the meeting I framed the problem carefully, let him know that he's a valued member of the team and that he has a spot here as long as he wants it. This is about his growth and his future. This got around him being defensive.

I had taken the time to get specific feedback from people he'd worked with over the past few years. I had examples of things I had seen myself. He took it pretty well, but was still somewhat shocked, still thinking of himself as a helpful and good coworker.

I told him that I couldn't see a way to get him on important projects or get him meaningfully promoted if he wasn't seen as a helpful and team-oriented employee, and asked him if that made sense to him. He agreed, knowing these were important values for our organization.

I gave him specific ways I thought he could change his behavior. I told him that this wouldn't be a fast thing to change and that I'd be willing to help. "Remember, it will take at least six months to change your reputation and perception, and have anyone believe it is a "new you" and that this is consistent for the future."

Result. Dave changed his behavior. It took some time, but I knew what I was looking for, and so did he. I can give you details if you would like, but the short version is that he really applied himself to it. In about three months other team members had made positive comments about him to me without my asking them, and he started to be put on the kinds of projects he wanted shortly thereafter. I'm very happy with the changes he made and glad to have been a catalyst in his success.

Chapter 10

Tell Your Career Story

What Is a Career Story?

Your career story is your showcase, constructed to improve communication and set the "conversational stage" for your interviewer. It tells what you do, who you are, what you value, why you do what you do, what your goals are, and (possibly most important) why the interviewer should care and want to hire you.

Your mission when you tell your career story is to do all of the following:

1. Relate all of the most important facts about your skills.

2. Humanize yourself to your interviewer.

3. Show some of your personality, your values, and your "soft skills."

4. Provide hooks that capture your interviewer's interest and prompt follow-up questions.

In a manner of speaking, you are inviting the interviewer into your career showroom. You're pointing out all the features and benefits of your path so far, talking about the remarkable journey that led to this remarkable person that is in front of them, and discussing all the refinements and experiences that led to the tremendous capabilities and skills you possess.

You want them interested enough to want to find out about details that are important to them—that is, to ask you questions that permit you to show them more of your value in areas of particular interest to the interviewer—and at the end, decide that you're the candidate they want!

Now they just need to get through those other pesky interviews and get back to the important thing . . . securing your services!

Another way to think of this is like decorating a holiday tree: you want the viewer to be absolutely delighted when they see it—to think, "Ooooooh! So beautiful!" right when they walk into the room! The whole thing has to work together. Part of that is having a consistent theme and beautiful, carefully selected ornaments. At any distance, the effort and care that went into this perfect display (your career, as understood by the listener) is clear and distinct.

As with holiday trees, the experience represents a beautiful accumulation over time. There are the ornaments that family members made when they were kids—some passed down through generations—the mementos from important vacations, and the keepsake reminders of people who have passed.

This may sound difficult—and it can be!—but it definitely gets easier with practice.

The more experienced you are, the easier it will be to make your career story about very meaningful accomplishments which connect directly to your aspirations. That also makes it easier to craft and tell your story.

If you are inexperienced or early in your career, your story may be about preparation and readiness to take on the challenge that this opportunity represents. That's also a good story to tell; it can be very engaging.

There are things that make writing a career story easier:

- First, there is a pattern and structure to telling your career story. I'm going to lay that out for you in the next few pages.

- Second, it helps to know your personal values, which you recorded during the exercises in Part 1.

- Third, you should know your strengths and opportunities from *Worksheet 3: Skill self-assessment.*

- Fourth, you should have several STAR answers that showcase the strengths from your self-assessment.

Overall your story will help you point, inevitably and indisputably, to the fact that you are the perfect candidate for the job.

Note: If you cannot build this case, perhaps you're not ready for the job yet. That doesn't mean you can't try to get it, or even that you'd fail in it if you got it. Just understand that you had better plan on a lot of hard work to prove that you were the right pick for it and to keep the job if you get it!

Your heroic journey

Joseph Campbell, an American scholar of myths and storytelling, created a detailed academic model with 17 stages describing what he called "the hero's journey."

We're going to boil this down for our use to these five parts, in the context of creating connection and shared understanding with an interviewer through your own story:

1. Your Motivation

2. The Learning

3. The Challenge

4. Your New Ability

5. Your New Role

This order isn't strictly required. You may, for example, talk about your new role first and then discuss the other parts (what it took to get there), if it fits the situation better.

Let me give you an example of how this has worked in my own life. I was interviewing for my first titled position as an IT Business Analyst. The core of that job (in my case) is to be able to understand a business need and a technology solution and to facilitate the collaborative work between the people with the need and the people who construct the solution. Sometimes this involves speaking very technically about computers and IT matters, and sometimes it involves diving deep into a business problem and finding the underlying cause of the problem. In the best cases it involves helping very different people work together successfully.

Here's what I talked about at my interview. I'm noting and separating the conversation into the narrative parts noted above.

Interviewer:

So, Ryland, we're going to get to specifics about the position in a little while, but can we start off with you telling me a little about yourself?

Ryland:

Thank you! I would love to.

(1) I guess the thing to tell you is I've always had an interest in solving problems and being part of the "aha!" moment for people. I started off in school thinking I wanted to be a therapist, and discovered that just wasn't right for me. However, I learned a lot in grad school that I still use today, such as how to create an operational definition of a problem, how to design metrics-based experiments, and how to interview people—open versus closed questions, reflection, that kind of thing.

After I left school, I had the lucky chance to pick up some database skills and landed doing work at BellSouth Telecommunications as an IT specialist. Part of my responsibility was to manage our ongoing work with our technology providers and ask for enhancements to our systems.

To summarize about seven years and three successive positions with Bell very briefly, my supervisors consistently told me that when I managed their technology requests from vendors they got better results and better delivery than they were used to. Over that time, I went from doing 80% hands-on technology work and just 20% handling delivery of vendor work, to about 20% hands-on and 80% writing requirements and handling delivery.

(3) My challenge has been that my job has always had a lot of different pieces in it that I really enjoy—technology and people, soft skills and hard skills. About a year ago I wasn't sure where to go next with my career. Nothing was leaping out at me, there was no clear path forward, and nothing that fit what I currently did as a job description but at "the next level." It seemed like what I was doing was parts of development, project management, business analysis . . . but I couldn't find anything that fit with that as a "next step" that would value all three parts the way I'd been doing them.

(2) I talked to several people I considered mentors—both in and out of the company. They gave me some ideas from their own experience, as well as what they found my unique strengths to be having worked with me. They asked me what I felt most happy doing, most satisfied when I do it. Least bored, as well—I hate it when my work becomes routine, I like things that are at least *somewhat* challenging!

(4) From that I've landed on business analysis as the right thing. This is because it lets me work with that "aha!" experience the most, really helping people solve their important business problems. I get to switch between people and technology work just when I'm getting bored with the one or the other. And since the problems will be new and different, because business is always changing, I'm thinking this is the right fit for me!

(5) So, what I'm trying to do now is take all the skills I have from technology, working with people, solving the right problem the right way, and make them into a formal position as a business analyst. I know I'm ready for it, and I'm hoping this position is that opportunity.

Now, a few things about constructing this story.

- Building this story took *active and attentive crafting*. What you just read is not what I started with, and it took several iterations to get to this point.

- Absolutely every word is true. I wasn't lying or puffing my skills in any area.

- I rehearsed this story out loud several times before I used it in an interview, and I modified it from interview to interview to improve on it.

Over time, I built in "hooks" or "leads" that would invite the interviewer to ask me questions, for which I had STAR answers prepared and ready. They might ask, they might not, but I was prepared either way.

I think the story meets our goals:

- It makes me a person, not just a candidate, and gives the listener an idea of my motivations, history, goals, and values.

- It shows some of my strengths and why I'm the right person to consider for the job.

- It provides several opportunities for the interviewer to ask about things that I really hope they'll ask about, because I have a STAR answer ready to showcase why I'm the right person for the job.

If you find yourself with a behavioral or skills interviewer, you're already set up for success. You've given them a good introduction that helps them find whatever they're looking to find.

If you have a social interviewer, you have set a context for them to get to know you that focuses on your job qualifications, not just on how much they like you. You might stand out more than someone who they simply like, because the interviewer both likes you *and* has an idea of your ability to do the job. (There are still no guarantees with a social interviewer. They might be looking for their next best friend, not a person to get the job done.)

The five parts of your career story

Let's examine each of these five parts so you can craft your career story. You should also use *Worksheet 6: Career story starters*, which has questions that will help you tell your story.

Remember, this is mostly about your past, and aspirationally about your future. This tells the story of the journey *that you have already been on*, and it is important to show where you are in the journey now.

The story starters, which are repeated here and on Worksheet 6, are to get you thinking about each part in your own life. You don't repeat the starters for an employer, they're just to help focus your thinking and surface that story part for yourself.

After introducing the five parts, I'll provide some brief examples of how each part contributes to your story.

Your motivation

Your motivation is the impulse that is driving you to seek new employment *now*. In stories, something in the life of the hero has *changed*, and necessitates the beginning of their journey. In some way, the motivation represents an aspiration or something missing in the life of the hero. The hero must take a journey, learn new things, change and transform to be able to overcome a problem.

Something I feel called towards is _____.

A challenge that I know I face in my life is _____.

I find _____ is consistently in my way.

Something I have always aspired towards is _____.

The learning

No one gets anywhere on their own; everyone learns from someone or something. Experience drives and creates learning. You may have learned from a teacher, at school, or otherwise. This is someone who equips you with some piece of knowledge or training that enables you to overcome your challenge. The teacher may have been an elder, mentor, or parent, and may not have known you were learning a powerful lesson from them.

You may also have learned from a book you read or an unusual experience you had, as long there was a real "light bulb" moment in it for you.

No matter what, the key thing is that it gave you knowledge you could apply to be successful in the future.

I often think of _____ because they taught me _____.

A lesson I have applied again and again is _____.

I'm so grateful that I learned _____; it has been so helpful.

The challenge

This is the hero's big moment—the moment that they slay the dragon, save the village from a flood, or pass the final test. The challenge can be a situation such as a certification test, a major project, or a rival company you beat for a contract. Any obstacle that you could only overcome by working hard and applying your learning is probably an example of a challenge.

Had I not overcome _____, my life would have been completely different.

I often think of all the preparation I did to achieve _____; it made all the difference.

I think my greatest challenge so far has been to _____.

Your new ability

By overcoming the challenge, the hero has proven that they have a new ability. They prepared, learned, and prevailed, and now this success has been earned and they can do something they could not have done before.

After I overcame _____, I understood that _____.

Now that I can _____, it has made a huge difference.

Once I had gained _____, I was able to make real progress.

Your new role

Having set out from home to pursue their motivation, learned something important, successfully applied that learning to overcome their challenge, and developed a new ability, our hero is *transformed*. They are different than before all of this happened. They are now able to live in a role and hold a position that is new. In legends, this typically enables them to solve the problem that drove them from their comfortable home in the first place. They can now serve their community in a new and meaningful way.

The essential thing is that *through their efforts and labors they are now different than when they started.*

If the hero went to college, they have passed their finals and they are now an adult and ready to work. If the hero discovered they were missing meaning in their life, they traveled, met people from places around the globe, learned things, faced their own fears in the wild, and now understand what is personally important to them and are ready to make peace with their family.

If slaying the dragon was the climactic battle in the movie, the new role shows that the hero understands what it means to be a dragon slayer and take a place in the community they rescued. Without change from where they started, there is no new role. The challenge isn't the reason for the trip, it is just the vehicle to achieve the new role.

After all that has happened, I'm now able to _____.

The biggest change was on the inside. Now I always feel _____.

All the learning and doing I've done has enabled me to give _____ to my community.

I'm proud that I can make a contribution like _____ today.

Career story examples

In practice, your challenge leads to the new skill. This can be difficult to express sometimes, so here are a few examples expressed in simple points.

You might be more elaborate when telling your story; I'm deliberately keeping this brief and simple for illustration purposes, showing you how each part of the story shapes the next part.

Project management

Your Motivation	To be a great PM and help people succeed.
The Learning	Learned from colleagues and senior PMs, studied PM books. Had critical moments with mentors.
The Challenge	Got thrown into a new project, 10 times bigger than anything I'd done before. Was concerned about how it was going to go.
The New Ability	Successfully managed the big project by applying the learning and working extra hours, consulting with mentors.
The New Role	Now that I've handled this and I can express what I did that was different, I am prepared to be a Senior PM.

Sales

Your Motivation	To earn new customers by solving problems by using the company's solutions.
The Learning	Early experience from the field, with great leaders, showed me that you have to really understand the customer, the product, and the company.

The Challenge	Starting with a new company is always difficult. Relearning those things to a significant depth is a skill I've acquired over the years.
The New Ability	I have a proven method of working to understand the customer and their needs, and I always start there. It leads me to success every time, and I've used it repeatedly in the last 10 years.
The New Role	I can step in quickly as a salesperson with your company, as I have elsewhere in the past.

Management, leadership, employee development

Your Motivation	To grow top talent and be part of a leadership team. Wanting to make a difference in people's lives.
The Learning	Mentors and experience have shown me that to make a difference you have to be invested in the success of your team and each person on it.
The Challenge	I supervised a team member who was unhappy at work. Nothing I'd tried before was working. I found I had to make an extra effort to connect with this employee and understand their career direction.
The New Ability	Now, I consider myself someone who considers the at-work and away-from-work lives of employees equally important. Having empathy for an employee's all-around motivation is a new perspective.
The New Role	I am able to function in new ways as a senior manager, having taken my understanding and ability to motivate team members into a whole new dimension. I can work with troubled teams and help make them effective.

You can try completing *Worksheet 7: Career story* now. If you're still unsure, the discussion of career archetypes in Chapter 21 may help.

Remember that your career story can take time to craft and you will likely revisit it several times. It will take work, and I encourage you to spend some time with it.

Get feedback about your story

Getting useful feedback about your career story can be difficult. You can use *Worksheet 7A: Career story feedback* to get listener impressions of what you said. You can use this to improve and refine your story and how you tell it.

Give the worksheet to a trusted person with whom you are practicing your story. Instructions are repeated on the page. Don't tell them what you have done to craft your story, just tell them the story. Let them have a few minutes to write down their reactions and thoughts, uninterrupted. Let your friend know that there is no right or wrong answer—this is strictly about what they understood from listening to your story.

Hopefully, they received what you intended to transmit! If not, you know what they did hear and you can discuss what you said that caused them to answer the way they did.

Remember: they are doing you a favor here. They are not simply "wrong" if they didn't have the impression you intended to create for them. Use this as good feedback about *your* communication abilities. Refine your storytelling and try the exercise again, possibly with a different person.

Know When To Move On

People can be dissatisfied with their job for any number of reasons. Some are good, solid reasons, and some are just reactions to an isolated bad day or a rough patch at work. It is often hard to figure out the problem from the inside, so I think that finding a way to take some of the emotion out of this decision is a good thing.

Framing the conversation

One of my former mentors, Barb, had a rule that's central to this discussion: "You can only evaluate something in the context of your next best alternative." (For more of Barb's Rules, see Chapter 13.) This discussion is built around that rule.

I also want you to use the tools and techniques in this chapter to help you take your ego out of the decision-making process.

Why? Because I have seen people pursue new work just because they were slighted by someone at their current job, though they won't admit it. The slight, or person, may be completely unimportant in a better light, but they focus on only the problem and decide their job sucks and they have to leave. That is a very expensive decision to make based just on one episode or interaction.

Worksheet 8: Thinking about a job change will help you structure your thinking and get all the pressure out of your head and onto paper. This will let you, and possibly very trusted others, consider your thinking and options.

Each of the items on this worksheet may be highly important to you or not important at all. I'm trying to prompt some thorough initial thinking; however, as with other items in this book, feel free to add or remove things as you see fit for your situation.

Remember that everyone will be different here. For example, some people enjoy job-related travel, some people hate it, and some people are willing to tolerate it. One person may absolutely want job-related travel—they love and expect it in their work! They will not be interested in any position unless it includes a lot of travel with destinations in many different countries. For someone else, any amount beyond occasional short trips is a complete deal-breaker. It is all up to you and what matters to you.

Reputation is another example of something that can be a pro or con. If you have done a lot of "growing up" at your current employer, or you've somehow become "unadvanceable" due to some negative event—real or perceived—you may need to change companies and start with a mostly clear slate. In this case, you're actively looking for that blank slate on which to create a new reputation. On the other hand, a new position always involves extra time and effort to prove yourself. For someone else, rebuilding their reputation may be a drawback. That person enjoys a good reputation and positive reaction whenever they walk into a room at their current employer. They will have to earn that all over again with a new one.

Using this worksheet

I've left the headings blank in the worksheet so that you can fill them in for whatever you're trying to do. (The sample shows one example of headings you might use.)

What do I want? What do I expect?
If you are dissatisfied with your current job but don't have another in mind yet, you can use this worksheet to evaluate what you have now and what you would want in your next situation. You can fill this out for your current position to figure out what you feel is lacking and what you want to be better in a new position. Consider what's negotiable for you and what isn't.

How good is this new opportunity?
If you have a new opportunity in front of you, you can compare your current position and the situation you're actively considering. Fill out what you know about your own job and what you *know, suspect,* and *believe* about the new one. This may help you come up with good questions to ask during the interview with the hiring manager or the recruiter.

What would it take for me to say yes?
You may use this worksheet to decide what would make you say yes to something. I encourage you to be fanciful but not outrageous in this case. For example, you might indicate you would certainly say yes to 150% of

your current wages, or whatever you consider a super raise for a new job. There's no reason to write down 10 times current wages if that's the equivalent of winning the lottery. Nobody turns down winning the lottery, so it doesn't help you answer this question.

What's in it for me?

When I have done this myself—and I have done exactly this, when looking at different positions—it often puts me in a much better frame of mind about my current job. One time, by going through this exercise, I realized that I already had a great position that I enjoyed most of the time. But I didn't have a challenging project. *I was bored!* So instead of changing jobs I found a project that would challenge me—once it was something at work, and a different time it was something outside of the office. Both times I was happy again and decided not to pursue another position.

Another time I went through this worksheet and decided that my issues weren't resolvable at the current job. I couldn't advance towards my big goals while at that company. I considered a lot of options and approaches that could change that situation. I checked my thinking with a few trusted people at the company and they agreed with me: my options were closed. Leaving was the right thing to do. I cast a net out there, and when the right opportunity came along I took it with no regrets.

What I'm saying is that you should carefully consider

- what you have,

- what you want,

- what is a realistic next step,

- what would be a golden opportunity you cannot pass up, and

- what would be an insufficient opportunity you simply should not take.

Once you work that out, you are well positioned to actively consider whatever comes your way. You won't be scrambling to consider what "good," "great," and "no way" look like, and you can focus on making the most of the opportunities that arise.

Chapter 12

Be Outstanding In Your Work

As part of my work on this project, I spoke with several people in leadership positions—senior director, vice president, C-suite—at both established companies and startups, and across several different professional fields.

I asked them what makes a candidate or an employee a *standout*. Someone memorable; someone they ask for on crucial assignments; someone they might even keep track of during their career.

Obviously, competence was a key criteria. The rest of what you do isn't important if you can't fulfill your job function. But there was a common theme beyond that.

The theme was *passion*.

When someone is passionate about what they do it shows in all of their actions. As one executive said, "When I know someone is passionate about their subject, I don't have to worry about them pursuing the goal. They overcome challenges, they problem solve, they innovate. They will achieve results. I don't have to spend much time monitoring or worrying about them."

One of my interviewees, a senior medical practitioner who also takes on trainees, said: "I don't care how much you know, until I know how much you care. Someone who puts the care of the patient first—above all else!—someone who is relentless in service of the patient. That's the person I want to train and the one I want working with my patients."

You can't fake passion for your work. You have it or you don't.

If you do try to fake it people will notice very quickly. I don't advise even attempting that: you will lose credibility. Nothing good will come of it.

You need to find out what you *are* passionate about, and try to work with that as much as you can. Remember our Zone of Awesome? Doing something you love—something where your passion shows—is part of getting to that zone.

This is one reason I suggest you find the thing in your career that you're passionate about and try to spend time with it. Over time, it will help you stand out. It will lead you to the things you love doing and care about deeply. You will easily have an engaging career story, loaded with STARs of huge relevance and interest.

You may have heard the saying, "When you love what you do you never work another day in your life." When you love what you do, your energy tends to automatically gravitate towards *advancing*—producing value and accomplishments in pursuit of your passion.

When you love what you do, you don't watch the clock. You don't pray for Friday. At the end of the day you wonder where all the time went because you've been doing things you love doing. You wonder how you're ever going to get all the things you want to do done if the time goes so fast!

It is hard to love *everything* about any job position. If nothing else, I'm sure you hate filling out a timesheet, or perhaps you have to suffer through a particularly boring staff meeting every week.

However, by understanding the things which you *do* love about your job you can try to work in a place of great satisfaction and engagement as much as possible. The rest becomes the cost of doing business, and you try not to focus on it. Don't let your suffering of the mundane destroy your joy of the exceptional.

Assuming those are important to your position, then you will stand out— and if they're not important to this position, consider looking for a new one!

Knowing what you're passionate about and being able to show work-related accomplishments can be very helpful to your career story. They'll help you be a standout candidate in your interview. A story that comes from your passion will flow more easily, be more relatable, demonstrate your values, and have a powerful kind of authenticity.

Being able to express your passion and be seen as working in it will help open doors that are related to it. As you do little things in your area, people will notice you. They will bring you things related to your passion because they know you're interested in those things.

Try to permit this and don't shoot it down: it snowballs if you let it! People begin to invite you into things which connect to your passion because of the contribution you want to make. Over time, this accumulates, and the circle broadens. You will probably be invited into interesting and exciting opportunities that you never even knew existed. This is part of the reason for spending time with your values, your goals, and in this case, your passion.

I'm speaking from direct experience about this: find some way to take action about your passion. It is a great thing to do.

Part 3
Lessons and Gifts

Introduction to Part 3

Everyone has lessons to learn, and I cannot guess what yours are. We all have different experiences and "teachable moments." I've had a few myself. In many cases, I was lucky to have things passed to me by managers, mentors, and friends.

As I mentioned in my preface, I want to honor those people who have invested time and care in me by passing that forward to you.

As you read this section you may be surprised at a mistake or problem I encountered. If so, take it as a good thing that you have already learned that lesson, hopefully without paying whatever price I paid.

I won't be offended if you read something and say "wow, he didn't know that?" or even think I must have been completely stupid to have needed that lesson. In an ideal world, everyone would already have had these lessons when they are inexpensive to learn.

I hope things are more ideal than I think, and that most of my advice here is stuff you already know.

Chapter **13**

Barb's Rules

At one time I had a friend and mentor named Barbara—Barb for short. She was an insightful, experienced, and tremendously talented human resources professional. She had led enormous organizations with great success.

She imparted to me good counsel that I now share with you as Barb's Rules.

Rule 1: About your supervisor

"The key determinant of your job satisfaction is your relationship with your supervisor."

If you and your boss get along well, you'll basically be happy at work. If not, you won't. This doesn't mean you need to change your job or your boss if you aren't happy; it does mean you need to carefully and consciously care for this relationship.

This has proven true again and again in my experience. Never underestimate this factor in your work, or in any job you may be offered.

Rule 2: About your alternatives

"You can only evaluate something in the context of your next best alternative."

You may love or hate your work, but when you're seriously considering a change you need to have your realistic next best options displayed for comparison. Without considering your options it is easy to jump from the frying pan to the fire, or to subconsciously give the message that you don't care about your job anymore when you just don't have a better option. Remember that you can use *Worksheet 8* to think about a job change.

Rule 3: About money

"Taking more money to keep a job you hate is like having your hand on an electric stovetop: you won't like it any more than you did before, you just have some rationale to tolerate the pain."

There are good reasons we might take a job that pays well when we hate the work. Probably, this is in the context of sacrifice towards a meaningful goal, such as putting a child through school, paying off a major debt, providing for a family member, or building funds to go independent.

You're still going to hate going to that job.

If you have a job that pays well and you hate doing it, and you're *not* sacrificing towards a goal, you should be looking to get out of there. Rule 2 applies to this, as does what is important to you. Go back and look at *Worksheet 1: What do you value in your workplace?*, and *Worksheet 8: Thinking about a job change.*

Rule 4: About the organization

"Long-term success with an organization depends on your values matching up with its values. You won't be successful without this."

This can be a more complicated rule to consider. It can be hard to identify your organization's values, and they can change with time and as leadership changes. Both of those changes will be slow, but they could be important. You will learn what the organization values by watching what the leaders and senior members of your organization say and do, what kind of people are successful in the organization, and which people are rejected by the organization and leave.

This takes time and observation. Don't expect to come by this information suddenly.

For example, let's say an organization values hierarchy, data-driven decision making, or strongly directive management. Your values are "leadership is not a level," gut-driven decision making, and management which is more supportive than directive. You may function and be effective in the organization, but those above you may or may not see you as "part of the team." Frequently (but not always) those in authority and power offer the "hand up" to people like them.

In my opinion, more enlightened and conscientious leadership will be more attentive to a diversity of thought and approach, and consider how individuals will contribute to the success of the organization. To be honest, this is *not easier* for those in the senior leadership positions, and not every one of them will choose such a path.

Consider a different example. One organization values effective outcomes, developing talent and skill, and collaboration. Another organization values effective processes, managing to a budget, and success over failure. Does one of these sets sound more potentially open to a broad range of personal approaches to leadership and work? I would think the first example would be more open than the second.

Knowing your values and the values of the organization you're in can help you consider your strategic plan with any employer.

Chapter 14

Reliability Is the Foundation of Work

I consider reliability the foundation of everything we do in life, including in the workplace. This is so simple that it often goes without saying; I prefer to say it, clearly, so we don't lose sight of it.

If you cannot follow these simple rules you probably won't be successful, at any level of responsibility, in any field:

1. Set expectations.

2. Meet expectations.

3. Communicate in advance if the expectations need to change.

Let's clarify these a little.

Set expectations

In every job, at every level, you have to accomplish tasks or meet goals. This always carries an expectation of the date and time by when you will complete them.

A goal can be as simple as "clean the floor, now" with the expectation that it will be done in a reasonable amount of time. Or a goal may be more complicated, like "distribute afternoon medications to all patients by 5 p.m. each day," or something longer term and self-managed like "have the first draft of the business plan ready in a week." This happens all the time, in every job. The more senior you are, the more independent action and self-direction is expected of you.

Your fundamental reason for being at work is to accomplish things. Your team—the manager, your coworkers, others in the company, and eventually the customer—are all there because someone expects some *thing* by some *time*.

It is important that you always know and communicate to those who depend on you what you will deliver, by what date and/or time. This is called *setting expectations.*

If the expectation is impossible to meet, you should talk about that fact with your supervisor as soon as appropriate and try to problem solve. Maybe they don't know about the other work you're involved in, or the task is easier than you think, or they have resources they can offer you to assist, or they can change the due date.

Meet expectations

Having set an expectation, you must meet that expectation. That is, you must successfully, and with appropriate quality, deliver the thing you said you would deliver by the moment you said you would deliver it.

This is called *meeting expectations.* It is the most basic thing you have to do in your work, no matter what that work is.

Meeting expectations consistently is . . . well . . . *expected.* By itself it doesn't make you outstanding. It is considered "table stakes" of being at a job. It is not worthy of commendation or promotion.

Done consistently it makes you *reliable,* which is still more than some people will do.

Consider unreliable people in your world. Picture how bad it is when you cannot count on someone to do what they say they will do—at home, at work, or when you purchase services. What happens when your electricity, your babysitter, a family member is unreliable? How about your bank or your doctor? What happens when things are packed and shipped unreliably? Your car not is not repaired at the promised time? Even when a pizza is delivered a half hour later than planned? You never forget unreliability.

Now, about that coworker you have to cover for because they can't be counted on to get their work done on time. How does that affect the team? How about the team manager? How does it affect the perception of your workgroup by other teams?

Being consistently unreliable is a career killer.

Communicate *in advance* if expectations need to change

If you have set an expectation and you know you will not meet it, you must tell the person who has the expectation, and you must do this *before* the date they expected the deliverable. Typically, an explanation of why this is occurring is expected as part of the information.

This lets the person expecting your deliverable deal with this situation and not be surprised by the problem at the last minute.

Typically, this is still not a good thing, but it does help to preserve your reliability: people know that you will do what you say you will do . . . and if you know you won't, they will hear about it *ahead of time*. If they don't hear from you they can make their plans based on you doing what you said you'd do. They can count on you being reliable.

Own your work, both good and bad

If you missed an expectation, *own it*. This is the cousin to reliability: *responsibility*. I like to say that you can't take credit for your good work if you won't own your bad work.

Have you met anyone who typically does good work but who can't admit when they've made a mistake? They act like everything they do is perfect. They're defensive about everything they do.

Don't be that person.

We all make mistakes. Treat them like you would as an adult at home: (1) apologize sincerely, (2) show what you will do to avoid the problem again, and (3) do what you can to make up for it.

There is an important aspect of responsibility that promotes your reliability: people know you will be honest with them. You'll tell them, for example, when a piece of work you're delivering on time has a defect that you couldn't avoid. You won't cover up mistakes or problems—you won't "pass the trash" and set them up for a problem without them knowing about it. They can trust you.

Reliability is essential

You must demonstrate and guard both your actual reliability and the perception of that reliability. It is a professional asset that you cannot do without.

Chapter **15**

"Flip the Script" About Job Hunting

I'm about to challenge some conventional thinking about how you consider a job.

I'm doing this because I want you to have the most possible freedom to achieve your career goals. Being able to think about something from more than one angle increases your freedom.

Nothing in this chapter should be taken as an endorsement to do any of the following:

- Show a big ego, brag, or otherwise adopt a lack of humility at an interview

- Act like someone is competing for your services

- Adopt a one-up position towards the interviewer, their company, or other candidates

I am specifically telling you to **NOT** do those things. Every one of those things is a good reason not to hire someone.

See abundance, not scarcity

In my opinion, many people who are looking for their next position are putting themselves in a one-down position, or coming from a view of scarcity. They think of themselves as just another person looking for a job—one of a sea of candidates that the hiring company can just dip into and pull one person out of. They feel like the jobs are few and the candidates are many and they should consider themselves lucky to even get an interview, let alone be offered the position.

This idea can come in grades of mild to severe for any person. In some cases and in some economies (such as a major recession) it may even have some degree of truth. However, most of the time, it is fiction. When unemployment in a given field is low (5% or less) hiring managers are not usually sitting on a tall stack of qualified applicants.

When I'm on the hiring side, I typically identify three key skills or abilities any candidate must have, and twice as many "nice to have" abilities that will help me start to rank candidates.

I'll tell you a secret: typically, almost every candidate has two out of three key skills—differing ones—and then I have to use my judgment about which one to take. I almost never see someone with all three "must have" key skills in serious quantity. Those "nice to have" second-priority items help create shades of better or worse fit, but they usually don't make it decisive. It still comes down to deciding on my top two or three candidates and then evaluating those.

It isn't apples-to-apples at this point! It is apples, oranges, star fruit, watermelons, and a bunch of grapes. All could be good, and I have to figure out what is best for the specific situation for which I'm hiring.

Sometimes I have four or five key things, and I still find most candidates are missing one of the items. It is *very* rare to find someone who has every ability I want at the level of skill that I want.

The lesson for you is this: in a good economy you have a chance to stand out somehow. So don't put yourself one-down on anything. Don't count yourself out too early.

Change your perspective

Let's flip the script. Assuming you can put your best case forward, you should start thinking about what this job offers you, in addition to what you offer it.

If this is a conventional employment position (not a contract job) you are probably looking for a place you can spend at least three to five years, possibly even all of your career, depending on the details of your situation. You are preparing to trade your time, energy, effort, and skills for whatever basket of goodies this situation offers you.

In other words, consider yourself a job shopper: you're going to "pay" for a job with your time, skills, and effort, and you want to go looking in the job store for the best deal you can find.

We tend to think of that simply as a salary rate, possibly a bonus, and whatever benefits package is offered. (This varies from country to country—in the United States, evaluating these will be different than in the Eurozone or Asia.)

These things—compensation and the basic structure of benefits—are more or less commodities: $80,000 from one company is the same as $80,000 from another company—the dollars aren't different. Depending on your location, benefits such as healthcare, tuition reimbursement and the like are fairly straightforward to compare. They have an easy financial evaluation; a company that offers $1,000 per year in tuition assistance is the same as a base salary of $1,000 more at a different company—if you're in school!

What else can help you distinguish between job opportunities you want and ones that are the same as everyone else? Here's a list of things you can consider:

- What is the quality of management or supervision you're going to receive?

- Is there anyone there you will learn from? How closely will you work with those people?

- How often does this environment promote from within?

- If you are in a professional specialty, is there a Community of Practice, a Center of Excellence, or something similar already organized there? How active is the group?

- Will you report to someone who is in your discipline or a generic "project team" manager? Who is responsible for writing your annual review?

- What are the typical working conditions of the position and company?

- How flexible is the schedule?

- Are they willing to accommodate your family or volunteer obligations?

- Is commuting a problem where you live? You may want to know about the company policy on teleworking. How common is it at the company?

- Is the person you report to a micromanager, or an active partner who eliminates blocks from your path?

- Is there a career path in this job?

- Are the company's values similar to yours?

. . . and the list goes on, according to your own interests and profession.

Make sure you are considering the full basket of features the company and position offers you. Some things are worth a lot of "generic" compensation, depending on how happy those non-financial things make you.

What to avoid, and what to try

You can get the same information in a lot of ways. Here are a few examples of things you'd like to know, with different ways to ask about them.

Does this employer have a Community of Practice or Center of Excellence?

> **BAD:** "Do you take [my profession] seriously enough to have a Center of Excellence?"

> **BETTER:** "I've always wanted to be involved with a Center of Excellence for [my field], and to help identify best practices and helpful techniques. Is this something you already have, or would there be any interest in starting one after I've become seasoned in my position?"

How much schedule flexibility is present?

> **BAD:** "I don't like to be monitored. Does this position permit me to come and go as I please?"

> **BETTER:** "There are times when I need schedule flexibility, typically for something family or medical related. Can I ask about what is considered acceptable here?"

Is there a career path?

> **BAD:** "I'd like to know that I can be promoted in the next two years. Can I expect that?"

BETTER: "A previous employer had a problem where we lost several long-term, talented employees because the company had no position to which they could advance. Is that an issue here?"

Is there employee development?

BAD: "As a manager, what are your strengths at developing your direct reports?"

BETTER: "I like to make sure I'm always growing as a professional. If my core job responsibilities become routine and are consistently covered well, would you, as my manager, be willing to help me find ways to grow new skills and experiences?"

If something is critical to you, then try a few ways of asking about it in advance of the interview until you can make it a useful question.

I hope these help you in creating a conceptual template to investigate the things that are important to you. You can always ask directly about something—just don't make it confrontational.

Ask questions, don't make demands

To repeat: Do not poison the interview. Do not come in with a big ego.

I am **not** advising you to walk in with a chip on your shoulder, telling the interviewer that they are competing for your services as an employee. That will quickly get you labeled arrogant, "not a team player," or worse.

I'm only saying that you should explore, diplomatically and appropriately, the things that are important to you **in a non-confrontational way** at some stage in the interviewing process.

Know your own value. Having a high value proposition to an employer is important. It lets you have different conversations with prospective employers. It gives you choices in the marketplace. Your questions about the workplace let an interviewer know that you take them seriously and are interested in the company and the position.

Chapter 16

Lynnette's Lesson

Early in my career at BellSouth (now AT&T) I was fortunate to have as my supervisor a lovely Southern lady by the name of Lynnette. I was a young professional (about 30), and she sometimes boasted that she was one of the very last people to work with the peg-and-cable switchboards. Shortly after she started, they went to electric switches and she changed departments.

At this point in my career I was a kind of technology generalist: I worked with databases and data, and helped my team get what we needed from our technology services teams. I was new, very inexperienced in my role (although I had the right skill set), and always afraid to show that I didn't know something, even when it had nothing to do with my job.

In short, I was an insecure young man trying to prove himself. I was succeeding at my core responsibilities, but I wasn't asking for help at the right times and on the right things. I was even sometimes defensive about it, and that is never a good thing!

After a few weeks of working with me, Lynnette sat me down to have a "good supervisor" talk and told me this:

> Ryland, I will never be the technologist you already are. I don't understand computers or databases and how to make them work the way that you do. And I don't have to, that's your job, and I know you can do it. I'm glad you're on the team.
>
> I have noticed you struggling to be everything to everyone, and in so being you aren't going to be good for anyone at anything. Nobody can succeed at everything, and you're no exception. The good news is that I don't need you to be an exception.
>
> My value is that I have decades of experience at this company. I literally grew up working the switchboards, and I moved into supervising people and handling projects of all kinds after that. I made mistakes and I learned from them, and I have had successes too. I know how this company works—not just the business, but the people. I know

all of the people in management and leadership positions across nine states. I've worked personally with many of the people who are now at the very top of the company. I know why things are the way they are, and how they got that way, and who cares about it, and that lets me smooth out a lot of problems for our team in advance.

That's part of my business value: deep and hard-earned knowledge of every corner of this company, built over more than 30 years working here.

Because I know from where I derive my value, I can be more free when I actually *don't* know something. I can admit it without feeling like I'm giving something away, without getting defensive, and without feeling like my job is being jeopardized or worrying that people will think less of me.

I don't expect you to bring the value that I do. You can't—you just simply *can't!* And that's OK because we don't need you to. We already have that by my being here.

What we need is someone who is good with technology. For our team that's you.

I know you're new. I know you don't know anything about the company and that you're going to have to ask questions. The rest of the team knows it too, and is happy to share their experience with you. They'll be happier—and you will be too!—if you say "I don't know about that thing, can you please help me understand?" when you don't know something. They do that with you, as much as they can, about the new capabilities you have brought to the team, because they don't know what you can and can't do for them, or how to do it.

I know you enjoy helping them learn, I've seen you be helpful to them. They would like the same opportunity. And, as your supervisor, I need you to allow that. I need you to say "I don't know" when you really don't know. It will let you get to the next level of your work and help you expand your own value.

I was very grateful that Lynnette took the time to have this conversation with me. It became the foundation of my work for the next few years: admitting what I didn't know became a strength.

What freed me to do this was being solid and competent on what I did know. In a way, that became my rock to stand on, my place of value, security, and solidity that I could operate from and admit when I didn't know something.

Know your value, and welcome help

Know what makes you valuable, and know that domain well. It frees you to be an expert on that and to admit you are not an expert on other things. Don't pretend to know things that you don't know. You won't fool anybody.

When you can appropriately say "I don't understand, can you please help me?" you create opportunities for others to show *their* value and to collaborate with you as a team member. You build connections with your coworkers by doing this.

Remember to show respect for the help they give you by paying attention to what they tell you—take notes if you need to—and to try to apply the gift of their knowledge. People probably won't mind repeating something once or twice . . . but not every time it comes up. Listen *and* learn.

Perhaps you have not needed a lesson like this; it may have been unique to me. In any case, I'm very glad to have had it, and I'm always grateful to Lynnette for being the kind of supervisor who was invested enough to sit me down and have the conversation.

Chapter 17

The Trust Equation

Related to reliability and responsibility, *trust* is a core concept in the workplace.

Trusted Advisor Associates has put forward a good way to unpack the idea. I suggest you check out their website (trustedadvisor.com) when you have a moment.

Understanding the Trust Equation

Figure 6: The Trust Equation

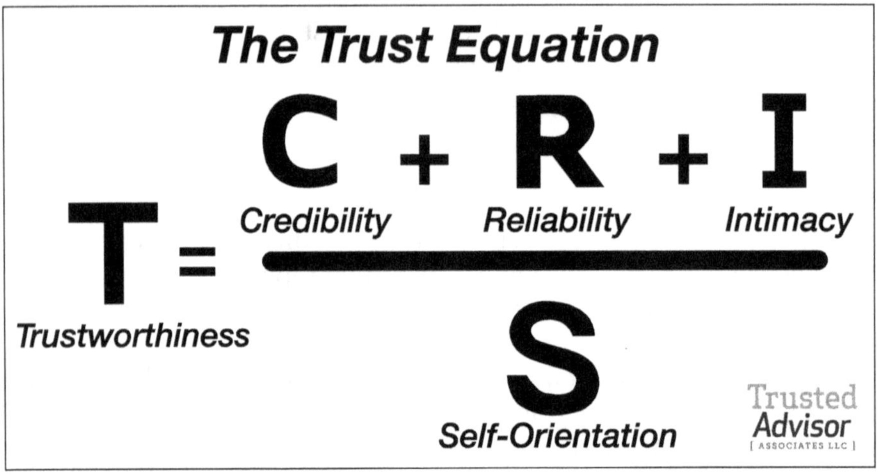

$$T = \frac{C + R + I}{S}$$

The Trust Equation

C + R + I
Credibility   Reliability   Intimacy

T =

Trustworthiness

S
Self-Orientation

Trusted Advisor [ASSOCIATES LLC]

The more self-oriented a person seems, the less we will trust them.

Source: The Trusted Advisor, Maister, Green, and Galford (Free Press, 2001). Reproduced from trustedadvisor.com courtesy of original author.

Like our discussion of reliability, this equation expresses something that we probably know intuitively, but it lets us think about it more clearly. Here are the parts, in my own simple definitions.

Trustworthiness

This is your ability to accept advice from, hold in high esteem, be influenced by, be relaxed around, disclose private information to, a specific person. Obviously, this list could go on for a long while.

Credibility

How skilled, competent, capable, trained, educated, or generically "good at" the thing in question is the person? What level of expertise do they have? What is their reputation?

Reliability

How consistent is this person at doing things that help you? How consistent is the quality of their work?

Intimacy

How "close" is this person to you? What have you gone through together? What is your history together? Are they in your inner circle or just an acquaintance?

Self-Orientation

How much is this person invested in their own well-being as opposed to yours? In your interactions, are they thinking of how this situation affects *them* or how it affects *you?* Are your interests or their interests put first? If there were a conflict in your interests, would they tell you?

Appraising trustworthiness

Look at the Trust Equation again. Trustworthiness is increased by the sum of a person's Credibility, Reliability, and Intimacy, *divided by* their Self-Orientation.

In short: *all other things being equal, the more self-oriented someone is, the less we will trust them.*

Imagine taking your car to a mechanic. You aren't a car person yourself, and you can't diagnose or fix the issue without them. You have to rely on the mechanic. They have done work on your car before (Intimacy) and they have diagnosed and fixed problems successfully in the past (Credibility, Reliability). You are set up to see the mechanic as very trustworthy.

They report that a small noise you're hearing is the timing belt starting to fail. If you don't fix it soon it could go at any time. If it breaks, the fix will probably be total engine replacement, which is hugely expensive. There is no predicting when it could happen: it could be next week, it could be next year. They won't guess beyond that. The timing belt repair is expensive, but a lot less than a new engine, and it's important to do it soon.

So far, how much do you trust your mechanic?

Now, let's add something to the situation.

How would any one item from the following list—just one!—change your perception of the mechanic's self-orientation?

- They are going through a personally expensive divorce.

- They are part of a team that rebuilds cars for charity auctions.

- They recently renovated their garage and waiting area.

- They are known to teach high school kids how car engines work.

And how would that one thing change your trust in this moment?

Trustworthiness at work

The same principle applies at work.

In the case of managers who practice any form of strong servant leadership, they must always and actively put the needs of others first.

In the case of peers, consider two coworkers who are credible, reliable, and intimate. One wants a lot of credit for helping you to be successful; the other is happy just to see you succeed and doesn't care about the credit.

Who do you trust more?

A final challenge

Of the coworker examples I just gave, *which one do you want to be?*

Chapter 18

Management, Leadership, and The Individual Contributor

I wish someone had explained to me, early in my career, the difference in career paths, trade-offs, and necessary skills between being an individual contributor and being a manager.

If you are an experienced professional much of this section will probably be old news to you; if not, I'm hoping I can give you some grounding in these ideas now.

Understanding the roles

First, let's define some terms. "Individual contributor" is easy to define. "Manager" is a bit harder. Entire books have been written about being a manager, management style, management activities, and leadership. I cannot possibly substitute for your own research in those subjects in accordance with your own interests and experiences.

Please read what I have to say, consider those points in the context of this book and then read widely should you need more information. I want to help you understand and consider these topics as you become a career explorer and consider your career paths and interests.

Individual contributors

An *individual contributor* (IC) directly does "the work." An IC does not supervise others, but typically works alongside other ICs. This can be in any profession. A few examples are accountants, software programmers, auto mechanics, plumbers, lawyers, therapists, carpenters, nurses, cooks, and so on.

ICs are responsible for the performance and outcome of *only their own work.*

In some cases this will be in the context of a team, with the team's performance shared by all team members.

ICs may tell someone else what to do from time to time, but they are not personally responsible for the work quality or work product of the other person. Typically, the IC receives an assignment from someone, does it, and goes on to the next assignment. In modern professional circles they will be expected to *collaborate with* but not *supervise* other people.

Managers

A *manager* is responsible for supervising a group of people (typically ICs) in service of an area of responsibility. Managers get their work done through others; the team collaborates to create the work product that a manager is expected to deliver. ICs on the team may have similar or different skill sets, but all are working to achieve the same ultimate team goal.

The manager is responsible for delivering that overall team goal and overcoming any problems that are in the way.

Management

Management is the activity of directing the work of ICs. Training people to do a job, directing tasks and assigning work, and ensuring that the team's work together is smooth and successful are characteristic activities involved in management.

Leadership

Showing the way, inspiring a vision, providing encouragement and support, and developing and coaching people are all activities of *leadership*. Any manager or IC can show leadership—or fail to show it.

There is a huge difference between being a manager and being a leader. Anyone can be given a management title. A reputation as a leader is always something you earn. No one can simply give it to you.

Very different career paths

If you are a new IC professional, I know, I know, *I know* that you are probably looking at managers and wanting that job someday. There are all kinds of things associated with it—authority, responsibility, and salary to name a few. It is alluring, and if you have any desire for recognition or career advancement you are thinking about it. It is an obvious thing to think about—everyone has a manager!

Being a manager is a different kind of challenge than being an IC. To be successful at management you must ultimately be more focused on others than on yourself. You will have more responsibility—though not necessarily much more pay—than an IC. Over time, due to being one step removed from doing the work, managers often lose the sharpness of their skills in their original IC field.

Some people love the challenge of management activities. Creating effective teams is a real skill and managers who have a proven track record of doing so are genuinely always in demand. Those managers almost always make a study of leadership along with their management skills.

As an IC you mostly get to do your work and go home. You don't have to worry about whether Debbie will be on time tomorrow, or Chris can handle that step-up project, or if you are relying on your star performer Erin too much and she's going to look for a new job, or how the quarterly team or company numbers are looking.

As a manager almost all of your responsibility is fulfilled through the actions of others, so those others move to the center of your attention. Their job performance, their job satisfaction, and their career growth are as important as the work assigned to your team.

If the team isn't delivering, then you aren't successful. It is that simple.

When you move into management, your IC skill set becomes "what you did before." You must quickly start over as a beginner at management.

Anyone can lead

Leadership is different from management. I am grateful to have learned that "leadership is not a level"—that is, it's not limited to the C-suite, directors, or your boss.

Have you ever had a coworker who could interpret what the boss said? Maybe someone who could tell you *why* what you were doing was important? Someone who helped you connect the dots about your job into meaning? All of these things helped you get your job done because you could see a vision of where you were going and what value it had.

That person was showing leadership. They helped you to clearly see a situation which had been cloudy to you.

Maybe you have gone through a change, such as a reorganization, that made you uncertain about the future of your work and someone talked to you about it. They had been through this before, and helped you see there would be some chaos but then people would settle down, and in a few months things would be running smoothly again.

That person also showed leadership. They encouraged you, and helped you find strength to get through a difficult time. They helped you do the same for others.

Perhaps in that same kind of situation you were not sure about how to help things improve—you wanted to make a difference but you were afraid of how others might see you or that they might think you were fighting the changes. Someone helped you find your voice, be constructive, dig in, and make a difference to the whole team.

That person showed tremendous leadership. They enabled you to make a difference to the organization and its goals.

None of these people had to be a manager or in a position of authority. They just used good leadership skills when the situation called for it. Leaders elevate others around them.

Everyone, IC or manager, should develop leadership skills to whatever degree they can. You will *always* be seen as a better coworker, employee, and candidate if you demonstrate leadership skills.

Considering management

Management skills are valuable, but try not to see a management position as a reward for being a good IC. That is an unfortunate and almost universal practice—great ICs are promoted to manage the people they used to work alongside, or a different team of similar people. If you don't *want* to be a manager, this can be a horrible situation for both you and the team.

If you are interested in management, make it part of your career planning. I also encourage you to know that your interest can and probably will change with time.

Your views and interest in management often adjust as you mature and as you progress in your career. This can be in either direction! I have met longtime ICs who decided on a management role, and I have met managers who similarly outgrew their role and decided to take an IC role. There's nothing wrong with either of these situations. They reflect different experiences, values, choices, likes, and dislikes.

If you don't know the answer, try to develop opportunities where you can find out more about management. These can be informal management positions, such as taking responsibility for a special effort on your team, or volunteer positions of management and leadership in a professional association or in your community. Taking on any of those things will help you answer this important career question.

We need good managers in the workforce

- Do you care about people and their professional well-being?

- Do you want to help people achieve their own goals?

- Do you want to make workplaces that don't suck?

- Can you develop and inspire people?

- Can you encourage their spirit and their skills?

- Can you organize them in service of larger goals?

- Can you do things you find personally difficult and challenging in the service of all of the above?

- Can you see yourself working hard at getting better at all of these things with time, making them a conscious practice and something in which you strive for excellence?

If you answered yes to all or even many of these questions, I *sincerely* hope you will consider management. It isn't for everyone! But if management *is* for you, then being a good manager will make a world of difference to the people you supervise. We all remember our good managers.

Career advancement as an IC

What if you decide management isn't for you? Simply put, you work to develop such a breadth and depth in your professional domain that you are incontrovertibly an expert on something. This will take time and diligence—but that is true of anything worth doing.

This kind of expert can think strategically and execute tactically. They can see the big picture and determine what course of action to take. They can explain their basis and conclusions to others and get buy-in for their proposed solution. They can execute and coordinate the activities necessary to achieve success. They can fluidly move between these activities as necessary.

Creating the next generation of practitioners is often the mark of true mastery of one's profession. An expert IC should expect to help grow and develop the talents of the other professionals in their field.

Leadership will become something you must demonstrate at need as a mature professional. Selected management skills will help, even if they are not a "core competency." Organizing and directing the work of people you are informally coaching and developing may be commonplace.

Some people are simply consummate and expert ICs. Masters of their art, they are brought in to solve the most difficult challenges in their field that a workplace can offer. This may be a temporary or permanent position, depending on the nature of the problem or field of practice. Someone who wants to be a non-leading, non-managing, narrowly focused expert on one thing is likely to work as a consultant who shifts from company to company as they solve that problem.

Chapter 19

Don't Date Your Job!

The relationship you have with your workplace is unique. The relationships we have elsewhere in our lives don't quite prepare us for this one. It takes time and experience to find this balance. I encourage you to give this active attention so you can keep the right mental footing about work.

Let me tell you about the moment this understanding arrived in my own life.

I was feeling crushed and hurt

I left work angry one day. When I got home, I started crying. It was over something hard to express, but I think many of us have been there.

I had made a request of my supervisor that I thought was a little out of the ordinary, but not unreasonable. It had been declined. I was shocked, stopped in my tracks, partly because I had been working *so hard* lately. I'd been putting in lots of extra hours, doing extra projects, taking on things I was told were critically important and had to get done, often in conflict with each other, and I was successfully getting all my work done and keeping my customers happy.

*I had been giving **so much** to my job and it had not given back to me.*

I felt horribly, horribly hurt for several days. I could not let it go, and I could not figure out why. By the end of it I realized the right words for what I was feeling were things like *heartbroken* and *betrayed*.

Let me be clear: my emotional reaction was irrational. I knew it at the time and I still could not shake it. The feelings were both deep and real.

I had the wrong relationship with my job

If the words I'm using lead you to think I was engaging in a highly personal relationship with my job, you're right. I was. And that's a big problem!

Your transactions with meaningful individuals in your life have a healthy reciprocity. Your friendships are there by choice, your family has a shared history, and your romantic relationship has a unique intimacy that should be of the utmost care and importance. None of these relationships are (I hope) emotionally one-sided.

Your workplace hits a lot of basic, critical needs in life. All of Maslow's levels are there: financial stability, well-being, pride in your work, enablement of your life outside work, and the fact that you probably spend more time there than with anyone or anything else in your life. It is a big deal. In the U.S., "What do you do?" is a common early question when getting to know people. It forms a big piece of our identity—frequently far too much.

And yet, the relationship with your job is *not* a personal one. It is not even a professional one. There is no other person in the relationship with your job. It has no parallel in our lives, and we often impose onto this professional environment the standards and expectations from our relationships with our friends and family.

The truth is that your job isn't in the same playing field as a relationship. Treating it as though it were is common but unfortunate and unhealthy.

You may have healthy, professional, constructive, respectful relationships with coworkers. You may have work friendships. You already know my views (see Barb's Rules) about having a successful professional relationship with your supervisor.

The crying, angry, hurt episode I described to you is not one of those. The facts of the situation were that I made an out-of-the-routine request at work and my workplace decided to decline it. There was nothing inherently malicious or judgmental about the decision. And yet, I got seriously emotionally hurt by this . . . as though I'd been told there was no trip to Disney World, or I was grounded, or even "no, I'm not free Friday night, and you know why!"

I was young, and it took me a while—and I mean weeks—to realize what had happened. Why I felt this way.

And it wasn't the fault of my workplace; it was my own.

Don't date your job

I was dating my job. Not my manager! I was dating the entire concept of my workplace—my job.

I sincerely hope you never do this.

It takes something that should be a simple transaction of the workplace and makes it something *more* than that, and that's where you'll get hurt.

You're engaging in an "inappropriate workplace relationship," but not the kind that HR warns you about! The problem is that there is no *person* on the other side of that relationship. You're making up things about how a nonexistent person should treat you! When they don't, you're hurt that the nonexistent person didn't do the things that you alone agreed they would do!

In any other relationship I've mentioned, such as friends or family, if you said something like "I helped you clean out your garage all last weekend, are you really telling me that you can't watch my dog for 2 days?!?" you might be reasonably upset and feel mistreated.

However, with the workplace, you can't say the same. "I've put in overtime and delivered twice the project load of any of my peers, on time and with quality, and you're telling me I can't have some schedule flexibility?"

Yes, they'll tell you that. And it could be for a good reason completely un-related to you as a person.

- Maybe the department is having an overall problem with work cover-age and no one is being allowed flexibility.

- Maybe your manager has already gone out of their way for you (pos-sibly without your knowing about it) and can't risk being perceived as giving you "special treatment," regardless of your performance.

- Giving you flexibility could show up on an upcoming audit and endan-ger your job.

Any of these could reasonably be true, or any similar benign and unrelat-ed reason that isn't personal to you and possibly wasn't communicated to you.

Yes, it could also be for lousy reasons. You may just have a poor supervisor who doesn't acknowledge and respect good work. Or their boss has some unreasonable goals for them and this is part of it. Or they aren't willing to go to bat for you about something. That definitely happens.

No matter what, getting angry about it and frustrated with it is one thing. Consistent treatment like this can easily make people look for other jobs, which is a reasonable and understandable reaction as well. But there's a difference between that and feeling like you're *heartbroken* at this kind of treatment.

Don't date your job. It isn't that kind of transaction. Take your ego out of the situation. This isn't about you and you shouldn't take it personally.

Once you do, you'll realize that you're behaving irrationally and try not to do it again. Then you can deal with the facts, evaluate them, and avoid reacting as if your job is an intimate relationship. It isn't. Don't give it that power.

Debbie made the same mistake

Over the years, I've had conversations with other people who have had the same experience. One stands out as a good illustration of this principle.

A good friend of mine, Debbie, was a senior manager in her organization. When her director, Frank, was promoted to a VP position, Debbie approached Frank and asked about the opportunity to apply for Frank's soon-to-be-former position, which would be a promotion. Frank knew Debbie was interested in advancing, and Debbie had been building a case for it for a long time.

Debbie had worked closely with Frank, had the right skills and knowledge, could step in with relatively little disruption, and had been a senior manager with the organization for several years in good regard. The organization also said they valued promotion from within, and acknowledged that positions above Debbie's were relatively scarce.

Initially, Frank told Debbie that he'd think about it and get back with her. About three weeks later it was announced that someone had been selected for the position. Surprise! It wasn't Debbie. Frank had not talked about this at all with Debbie, and after the announcement he couldn't find time to have a conversation with her and explain what had happened.

She later heard through the grapevine that her name had been put forward and rejected for unspecified reasons. She had not been allowed to make her case herself, interview for the position, or answer challenges to her qualifications. She had been completely stonewalled. She also assumed it wouldn't be the last time. She believed her future with this company was closed.

There's no question Debbie had been treated badly. Frank had shown his true colors here, and the personal let down was as significant as the professional one. It took Debbie literally a couple of months to get over this. She used many of the same words I'd used: betrayed, heartbroken, and abandoned.

As you might expect she decided to look for work with a different employer. In a few months, she'd found an opportunity with a new company that was exactly in alignment with what she wanted her next step to be. Right company, right position, right team, right compensation. She simply should not turn this down.

The language she used in her conversation with me about leaving included phrases like "I'm concerned about leaving them at a critical time," "I'm not sure how they'll get through this project," "I'm concerned about hurting their feelings."

At this point the "dating her job" aspect showed itself clearly. She felt guilty about giving standard and appropriate notice when she landed her new position with a new employer. She felt like she was somehow being disloyal even by looking for a new job at all!

She wasn't. That workplace—in this case, the people in it—had not treated her with appropriate respect and consideration. She didn't owe it to them to "stand by them" in some unnamed way. Unless you have a contractual obligation to give more notice, or you're in an industry where there is a special standard due to impacts on vulnerable people (medicine, law, possibly others), two weeks is the conventional expectation in the U.S.

(I'm aware this is different in Europe; the social contract about work is also more balanced in Europe.)

She had been having a relationship with her job. Now, she was having a hard time breaking up with it.

Do great things, just keep your boundaries sensible

As I said in the preface, my wish for you is that you might follow your passion, take pride in your work, deliver great value, and always do the right thing. Be happy, satisfied, and proud of your career as a whole. Care for and respect your workplace, your coworkers, your supervisor, and especially anyone for whom you have responsibility. Treat your customers well. Do powerful and wonderful things at work, contribute to the company, and grow your skills, your abilities, and yourself as a person. Enable and support other people along their journey to accomplish these same things.

Value the relationships you build with other people and always act with integrity towards them.

Just don't date your job. It's a mirage that cannot care back for you.

Chapter **20**

You Are Your
Own Company—Always

When someone asks, "who do you work for?" I sometimes have a moment where I hate the question.

This is because no matter where I work, the answer is the same: I work *for* me or *for* my family. I work *at* a company, or *at* an employer.

Who gets your paycheck? Does your employer get it? No, you do. You spend it. It is the fruit of your labor.

You need to treat yourself like a business. That means giving thought to these questions.

What do I sell?

Know what you're selling. This can be your distinct set of professional skills and abilities: your ability to sell, paint, write, coach, manage people or projects, lead, perform nursing or accounting tasks, or anything else.

Know what value an employer gets from it. Know it the same way that someone selling furniture knows all the aspects of that couch in the showroom, the way the person at the electronics store knows everything about the phone you're looking at, the way a car dealer knows all the reasons to buy this car or that one and at what price!

Note that I said "skills and abilities." Your professional skills may be the same as other people's. Include things that make you stand out such as your passion, your ability to lead, or your community connections—whatever sets you apart from the "commodity professional" of your field.

Who are my customers?

To define your customers, start by asking "Who will pay for my product?" What kinds of employers would be interested in your services? If you're a nurse, the answer is likely hospitals or smaller institutions. If you're an accountant, it might be something broader—an entire industry relevant to your unique experience, such as construction or software. And so on for software professionals, painters, administrative assistants, and everyone else. At the "macro" level, what kinds of employers would buy your services? Are your job opportunities limited to companies of a particular size?

Second, "who are my customers?" means "who do I keep happy at my job?" In an employment situation it's important to know who benefits from your work so that your reputation—your brand!—is held in high regard. Sometimes, this means keeping your supervisor happy: solving problems for, and providing value to, the person who signs your annual review is an important thing to get right! This is the "micro" level. Depending on your situation, you likely also have to please the public, or whoever receives your services in other departments at your company. You want those people walking away from an encounter with you as satisfied customers—whatever that means in your role!

What is a fair market price for my product?

Think about all the research that goes into the pricing of anything you buy. Cars, toasters, cereal, coffee—they all have a price. There is a "commodity" price you pay for the average employee in a field, and there are entry-level and premium prices for new and experienced individuals. Know the typical rates for people in your field so you know what you can expect from an employer. This is also good input into your thinking about how you get premium prices for your work, by developing the attributes that make you someone considered highly valuable.

What is my value proposition?

Next, ask what problems you solve for an employer. What benefit do they get by having you there? This one can be a little tricky if you're not used to thinking this way. Here are a few examples:

As a project accountant, I ensure that you always know the accurate status of expenses and income on the project(s) in my care. I provide monthly tracking and summaries of these projects so project managers can stay on track and make corrections. I flag questionable or unusual expenses to management.

As a database developer, I design and create high-quality custom systems for use in storing and serving customer information.

I collaborate with team members to create working products that create revenue for the company.

As a company recruiter, I identify and acquire highly skilled professionals of all stripes for the company. I work to ensure that the individuals we hire are of the highest skill level, best fit background, and right knowledge areas, so that the company gets the highest return on the investment of the salaries and time we commit to our employees.

How do I stay current?

Most professional fields do advance and change with time. If yours does, and you don't, and anything causes you to need a new employer (layoffs, or relocating for personal reasons) you may have a problem locating a new job at the same wage level. Consider a more material consumer product. Refrigerators, toasters, phones, smart tech of different types—all advance with time, and it is likely that your profession does as well.

You should keep watch on developments in your field. Know what skills and abilities employers are looking for in regards to those things in order to stay competitive. During an economic downturn, this can decide whether you keep your job or not. And, if you should happen to lose yours, whether you can find a new one easily!

Who are my competitors?

When applying for a position, you probably won't know the other candidates under consideration. You can probably make reasonable guesses about the kinds of people and backgrounds they might have. Considering what they might bring to the table will help you make a compelling value proposition. It comes back to setting yourself apart from the "commodity" professional in your field.

Chapter 21

Career Archetypes

It may help you, perhaps just as a thinking exercise, to consider the kinds of people you've met in your life and work.

Does anyone come to mind in response to any of these words?

- Teacher

- Expert

- Curator

- Craftsman

- Visionary

- Strategist

- Artist

- Champion

- Networker

- Diplomat

If you have a clear idea of someone in response to that one word, you may have a good model for someone who fits an archetype in your mind.

Figuring out your own descriptive archetype may help you write your career story. It's a little like figuring out your personal brand. And, like many brands, it is something you can strive for, and usually something you *earn*. People know it or figure it out about you without you telling them.

You can always try to cultivate the brand you want through your conscious actions and words. You can influence your brand, but you can't have one that is far from the truth. People can tell, the same way they can with products on the shelf.

An archetype can serve as a unifying thread for the five parts of your career story, and it gives you a way to show your values, your consistency, and what you've been building towards. Since the best predictor of your future behavior is your past behavior, showing that your archetype is something positive and is core to how you operate is very important. A prospective employer can expect similar from you in the future.

Examples of archetypes

Let's take the word *teacher*. Synonyms could be mentor, coach, advisor, guide, or guru. If someone in our workplace fits this word, it sums up their behaviors, attitudes, accomplishments, motivations, and values.

You may say to someone at work, "Ted, he's such a, well, you know, a *guru* about (whatever)," and everyone nods and agrees. Everybody knows that Ted is the go-to guy about this thing, and that his input on it is accessible, valuable, and sought after.

You know that you can't figure out who to talk to about an issue you're having with a team in a part of the company you've never worked with before. You do know you should just ask Margie, because Margie knows everyone in the company. Margie probably fits the *networker* archetype.

Here are a few ideas for archetypes that might be useful at work. As with many items I've presented to you, these are a starting place. Add to the list, blend ideas from different archetypes, and create your own as you need to. You are looking for the thing that connects the things you do and/or why you do them.

The Expert [on a subject]	The person who knows everything about this subject. The absolute go-to person if you need help or knowledge about it. The subject could be a skill, a technology, an operational issue, or the history of a department.

The Mentor (or Coach)	The person who is known for helping develop others. They are known for being the best chance at turning around a troubled employee, and bringing out the best others. They have raised some of the top employees in the company.
The Great Communicator	When you have to figure out how to say a thing, this is the person. They have mastered messaging and finding the essence of any communication. They create awesome, clear, and memorable verbal and written communications. They are comfortable on stage or in front of groups at any time.
The Networker	This person knows everyone, what they do, how they got their job, and what they've been doing lately. They're plugged into the company grapevine. They know people at other companies as well.
The Curator	This person is always reading about one or more subjects, and keeps up on the latest and greatest thinking about things. When you mention something, they have several articles for you to read—and amazingly, they're relevant and useful! They may not know something themselves, but they know where to find it.
The Visionary	This person knows how to paint a picture of the future that instinctively connects with people. They can see over the next hill, take you on the trip, and make sure you're prepared to be successful when you get there.

The Politician	This person has a massive and deep knowledge of the people side of business. They immediately see what motivates an individual or group and speak to them in terms they will understand and with which they will connect. They succeed at getting agreements where others typically fail.
The Workhorse	This person is reliable; they not only get things done, they get a lot of difficult things done! They are known for being the go-to person for hard assignments on short timelines, and for reliably turning out tons of high-volume and high-quality work.
The Motivator	This person can inspire and excite people. They can find the right thing to say to get a demoralized person or team up and running again. They can tell you about the pot of gold at the end of the rainbow and make you want to chase it!

In the traditional use of the term, each archetype has a "shadow" side. This is another way of saying that sometimes our greatest strength is our greatest weakness.

Your archetype can take time to develop and is typically earned through actions and experience, which can make it harder to build or identify early in your career. If nothing in this section sparks a clear theme that applies to you, don't worry about it. You can still build an excellent and useful career story without one!

Afterword

Thank you for your time spent reading this book. I hope it has added something useful and helpful to your career journey.

Remember, as I've said several times, you may change your direction, your goals, and what you find important as your career progresses and as you learn and grow as a person and a professional.

I hope you embrace that change, learn from your experiences, and always stay open to the unexpected opportunities that pop up!

Please feel free to let me know what difference this may have made to you as you care for and progress in your own career through my website at **RylandLeyton.com**.

About the Author

Ryland Leyton has been working with people and technology since 1990. He loves being part of the "Aha!" moment that gives people new insights and experiences and teaches them things they can immediately apply.

An author and speaker who loves to inspire, enable, and empower, he has been teaching for over 20 years on technology and career topics. His work in any field typically involves taking complex ideas and making them easier for others to understand and use.

Professional speaking & workshops

If you've enjoyed this book, you may want Ryland to speak or conduct a workshop for your workplace, event, or professional organization!

Audiences love Ryland for his effective and engaging presentation style. Conference attendees describe him as an expert who is simultaneously approachable, engaging, personable, and entertaining. He emphasizes audience interaction, giving personalized answers to questions and often drawing on his own real-world experience to keep the conversation engaging and memorable.

Contact information

You can contact Ryland via his website, **RylandLeyton.com**.

Worksheets

The following pages contain the worksheets in a format that should be reasonably photocopy-able. You are granted permission to copy only the worksheet pages, including the example pages, for your own use, as often as you would like to!

Remember, you're going to revisit your plan, career story, and so on from time to time. Expect and embrace change. Don't let the you from five years ago make locked-in career decisions for you today.

I encourage you to register using your email at RylandLeyton.com. This will allow you to download the most up-to-date version of these pages as I make edits and improvements after this book is published.

I'm really not a spam risk: as of 11/1/2019 I have been collecting email addresses for about four years and sent exactly *zero* emails so far.

I expect to have a policy of sending no more than two per month when I do start using that list, and you can always unsubscribe if you find them uninteresting.

Worksheet 1:
What do you value in your workplace?

Being content with my work	
Having major accomplishments	
Being well-liked	
Being creative	
Serving others	
Having authority over others	
Inventing something new	
Advancing my career	
Making my own decisions	
Being competitive	
Having high income	
Having status	
Choosing my work location	
Having interests outside of work	
Being self motivated	
Being loyal at work	
Challenging myself athletically	
Challenging myself intellectually	

Feeling needed and appreciated	
Pursuing excellence	
Having low work stress	
Spending time with family and friends	
Helping society	
Having time freedom	
Collaborating with colleagues	
Working for the environment	
Being well known	
Having power	
Being independent	
Having job security	
Taking risks	
Being active in the community	
Gaining new knowledge	
Influencing others	
Being part of a team	

Worksheet 2: Goals pyramid

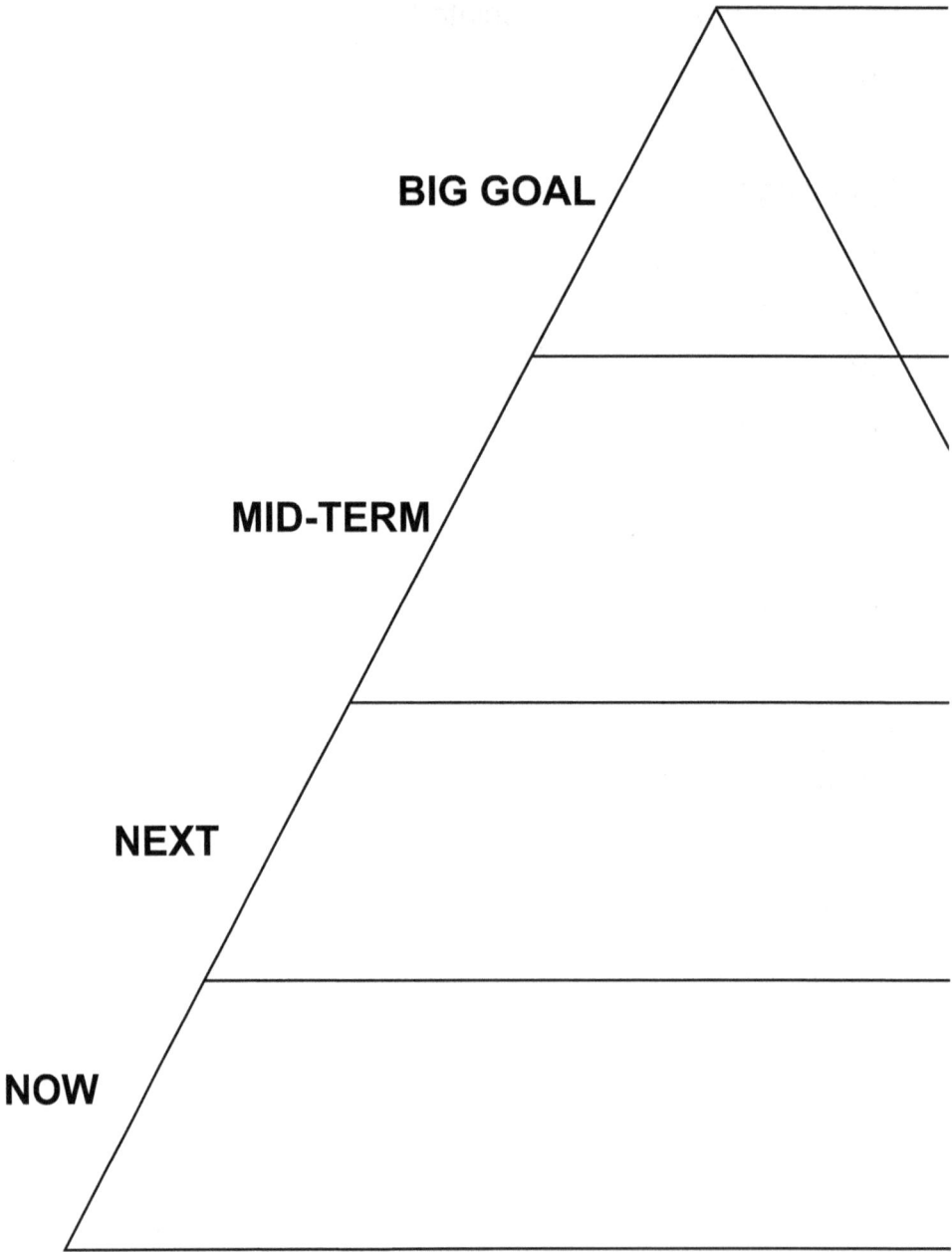

BIG GOAL

MID-TERM

NEXT

NOW

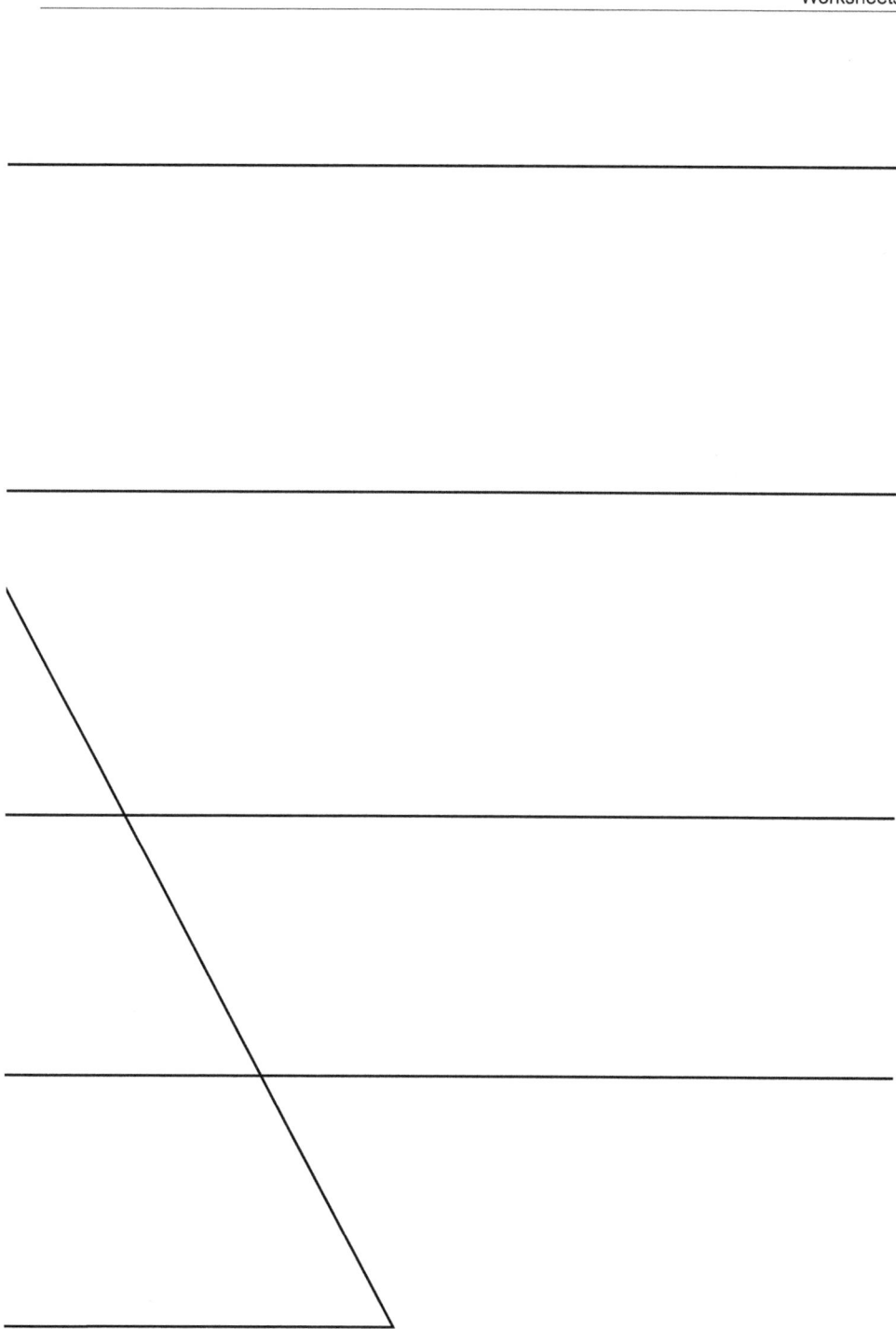

Worksheet 3: Skill self-assessment

Targeted Goal or Job: _____

Item or Area	Rating	What does this support?

Needs action?	What are possible next steps that help me meet my goals?

Worksheet 3:
Skill self-assessment (samples)

Targeted Goal or Job: _____

Item or Area	Rating	What does this support?
Able to facilitate meetings	4	Being seen as effectively coordinating and leading others.
Ability to think abstractly, identify patterns, generate ideas.	8	I want to be seen as a highly talented business-oriented problem solver.
Leadership skills	6	I am an emerging senior professional. I have demonstrated leadership skill.
Project planning	8	I am highly experienced at this with several examples.

Needs action?	What are possible next steps that help me meet my goals?
Y	Set aside time to plan meetings. Always publish a draft agenda with the meeting invite. Start shadowing people I think are good at this?
N	I need a way to showcase that I'm good at this. Find someone to partner with on an "extra" project? Talk to my boss about possibilities.
N	I have examples of this to draw on already. Keep building them, never hurts to grow in this area.
Y	Create a catalog of my projects. Find project testimonials of selected examples. Find metrics about outcomes?

Worksheet 4:
Your resume – professional experience

Company Title Dates of employment	
The "So What" of this position	
Summary of responsibilities	
Your accomplishments (3–5 bullets)	

Company Title Dates of employment	
The "So What" of this position	
Summary of responsibilities	
Your accomplishments (3–5 bullets)	

Worksheet 5: STAR answers

The thing I'm trying to illustrate or demonstrate:	
Situation • Context • Framing • Setup	
Task • Objective • Goal • Event	
Action • What I did • What I said • Skills I used	
Result • Outcomes • Achievements • The difference	
"So what?"	

Worksheet 6: Career story starters

YOUR MOTIVATION

Something I feel called towards is _____.
A challenge that I know I face in my life is _____.
I find _____ is consistently in my way.
Something I have always aspired towards is _____.

THE LEARNING

I often think of _____ because they taught me _____.
A lesson I have applied again and again is _____.
I'm so grateful that I learned _____; it has been so helpful.

THE CHALLENGE

Had I not overcome _____ my life would have been completely different.
I often think of all the preparation to achieve _____; it made all the difference. I think my greatest challenge so far has been to _____.

YOUR NEW ABILITY

After I overcame _____, I understood that _____.
Now that I can _____, it has made a huge difference.
Once I had gained _____, I was able to make real progress.

YOUR NEW ROLE

After all that has happened, I'm now able to _____.
The biggest change was on the inside. Now I always feel _____.
All the learning and doing I've done has enabled me to give _____ to my community. I'm proud that I can make a contribution like _____ today.

Worksheet 7: Career story

MOTIVATION	
THE LEARNING	
THE CHALLENGE	
YOUR NEW ABILITY	
YOUR NEW ROLE	

Worksheet 7A: Career story feedback

Work with a friend. Tell them your career story just like you would
at an interview: don't tell them the parts, just talk!
Afterwards, give them this page and see if they can answer the questions.

What inspired this person?	
What did they have to learn, and who did they learn it from?	
What challenge have they overcome?	
What did they achieve?	
What skills and abilities do they have now?	

What 3 words summarize your impression of this story?

1._____   2._____

What might a hiring manager be concerned about when hearing this story?

3._____

_____

Worksheet 8: Thinking about a job change

What are you comparing?	
TANGIBLES	
Wages *Hourly or annually*	
Bonus pay *Commissions, incentives, etc.*	
Health & Wellness Benefits *Quality of the plan, as well as costs*	
Long-term incentives *Stocks, discounts, or similar*	
Retirement benefits *401(k), pension program, etc.*	
Paid time off *Vacation, sick, family, etc.*	
Product Discounts	
Educational benefits & reimbursement *Tuition or book reimbursement*	
Professional development *Expenses, time off, conferences*	
Company training *How often? What kind?*	

What are you comparing?	
INTANGIBLES	
Professional advancement	
Work you enjoy doing	
Relationship with supervisor	
Professional network inside company	
Your reputation at the company	
Reputation of the company *Does it help you in any way?*	
Commuting *Time, transportation mode*	
Job-related travel	
Schedule flexibility	
Work/Life balance	
Job security/stability	
Consistent vs. new & different work *Is the work routine or changing?*	

What are you comparing?	
CONTEXTUAL	
Industry you care about	
Aligns with your goals	
Aligns with your values	
Company size *Small? Large? Private/public?*	
Social investment of the company	

Worksheet 8:
Thinking about a job change (sample)

What are you comparing?	CURRENT POSITION
TANGIBLES	
Wages *Hourly or annually*	$75,000.00
Bonus pay *Commissions, incentives, etc.*	10% ($7.5K)
Health & Wellness Benefits *Quality of the plan, as well as costs*	Family coverage ($250/month
Long-term incentives *Stocks, discounts, or similar*	No
Retirement benefits *401(k), pension program, etc.*	Yes (vested) Matches first 6% at 50%
Paid time off *Vacation, sick, family, etc.*	4 weeks
Product Discounts	No
Educational benefits & reimbursement *Tuition or book reimbursement*	Degree: $3,000/year with at least 3.0 GPA Books: $500/year
Professional development *Expenses, time off, conferences*	Up to a week a year time off
Company training *How often? What kind?*	Promised; never happens (Budget)
Conferences	No
Memberships, Subscriptions	$200/year reimbursable

I WOULD DEFINITELY SAY YES	THE THING I AM CONSIDERING
$90,000.00	$85,000.00
15% ($13.5K)	10% ($8.5K)
Same or better	Family coverage ($200/month)
No	No
Same	After a year, matches first 4% at 100%
4 weeks	3 weeks (+1 after 5 years)
Same	No
Nice, but I'll take salary instead	$2,000/year with passing grades; no books
Would really like 1/year	
Same	None

r

INTANGIBLES	
Professional a advancement	Yes, but I'd have to change dept.
Work you enjoy doing	Yes, but I'm bored.
Relationship with supervisor	Good
Professional network inside company	Good
Your reputation at the company	Good
Reputation of the company *Does it help you in any way?*	Good company
Commuting *Time, transportation mode*	35 minutes, and near kids' school
Job-related travel	Very rare
Schedule flexibility	Up to supervisor (OK)
Work/Life balance	OK
Job security/stability	Stable, been there 5 years
Consistent vs. new & different work *Is the work routine or changing?*	Work has gotten routine

Would like a career path	They say they have one
This is a must	I think I'll enjoy it
	Supervisor seems like he'll be OK
	None yet
	Need to develop this
	Good reputation
About 30 mins, near school	30 minutes, not near school
Same	None expected (rare)
Medium	Said yes to what I asked about
I'd like to stop on-call work	On-call once per quarter, expected
Stable company	Seems OK
	Will be new!

CONTEXTUAL

Industry you care about	Not really
Aligns with your goals	Used to, doesn't now
Aligns with your values	No, but not against them
Company size *Small? Large? Private/public?*	Large, Private
Social investment of the company	1 volunteer day/year

Not important	Not important
Really needs to	Does align
Would be nice	Seems OK
Any	Medium-sized, growing, private
	1 volunteer day/year

www.ingramcontent.com/pod-product-compliance
Lightning Source LLC
Chambersburg PA
CBHW070442090426
42735CB00012B/2443